DOUBLE HEADED

DOUBLE HEADED

Two Generations of Railway Enthusiasm

Gilbert Thomas and David St John Thomas

Drawings by Kenneth Lindley

DAVID & CHARLES

Newton Abbot   London   North Pomfret (Vt)

British Library Cataloguing in Publication Data
Thomas, Gilbert, 1891-1978
    Double headed.
        1. Railroads – Great Britain
        I. Title   II. Thomas, David St John
        385'.092'2   HE3018
        ISBN 0–7153–8184–9

Library of Congress Catalog Card Number 80-85490

First published 1963
Second impression 1981
Library of Congress Catalog Card Number

Printed in Great Britain
by Redwood Burn Ltd Trowbridge & Esher
for ·David & Charles (Publishers) Limited
Brunel House   Newton Abbot   Devon

Published in the United States of America
by David & Charles Inc
North Pomfret   Vermont 05053   USA

CONTENTS

CONTENTS

ILLUSTRATIONS

(This list does not include the numerous drawings by
Kenneth Lindley)

LIST OF ILLUSTRATIONS

PART ONE

BY GILBERT THOMAS

PREAMBLE

It is pleasant for father and son to appear within the covers of one book, of which the son is also part-publisher. It is pleasant, at any rate, for the father; and though I plead not guilty to having had any share in originating this volume, I have been a ready accomplice in its execution. For some readers the reflection of a strong family tie may have incidental appeal, as may evidence that the amateur interest of one generation can become an expert and professional interest in the next. But there must be more solid justification for making another addition to railway literature, and I hope it may be found in a picture of the changing face of our railways since the late 1890s.

Throughout my younger days there seemed no threat to the railway's complete sovereignty. The next quickest means of transport on land was, as from time immemorial, the horse. For journeys of more than a few miles the rich, no less than the poor, had to use what was still called 'the iron road'. Sixty or 70 miles an hour, with occasional spurts beyond that, was the highest speed yet attained by man, and an express train in full career remained the universal symbol of power. Nor, of course, did railways then seem plebian, any more than did trams and buses. In the country there were necessarily more private vehicles of one kind or another; but only very few urban families—mostly those of the old aristocracy—had their own carriages and coachmen. The rapidly-growing class of well-to-do manufacturers or tradesmen would have deemed it both unwarranted financial extravagance and a kind of 'sissiness' or ostentation to use other than public transport— when they did not walk—between home and factory, office or shop. And, as I have said, they had no option but to travel by train when distances of any length were involved.

Railways set the pattern of our economy and our lives. There is a sense in which the railways *were* Britain. Everything revolved around them, and their activities extended far beyond their own immediate role. They operated most of the ships connecting our shores with the Continent and with Ireland; they owned docks and harbours; they were the largest proprietors of hotels. They were Very Big Business, and the Annual Reports by the chairmen of the major companies were barometers of the state of national trade, and, as such, were studied with particular care.

If, however, the railway enjoyed a monopoly, competition between the individual companies prevented the dead hand. Here and there a line held virtually undisputed sway over the territory it served. One such line was the North Eastern; another was the Great Eastern. The NER, to its credit, took no advantage of its position. Its standard of passenger comfort was second only to that of the Midland; its freight service— the company pioneered in introducing larger than the normal 8- or 10-ton wagons—was extremely efficient. Moreover, the North Eastern was the first railway to inaugurate a staff training scheme, and, for many years after the line lost its own identity, ex-NER men were prominent in railway reorganisation all over the country. Their influence still lives on. The

Great Eastern, a poorer company, did not similarly shine, though before the first world war, under a general manager brought in from across the Atlantic, its London suburban service, if still steam-operated and relying on primitive four-wheel coaching-stock, was to become an acknowledged triumph of organisation.

In wishing to reduce competition the railways themselves were ahead of public opinion. Early in the new century the South Eastern and the London, Chatham & Dover companies were allowed to be run, as the South Eastern & Chatham Railway, by a joint committee; but when other, more prosperous lines wanted to combine, Parliamentary consent was refused. Later some 'take-overs' were permitted. The Midland swallowed up the London, Tilbury & Southend system, thus removing from St Pancras the beautiful green of the sturdy LTS tank engines which, together with the resplendent blue locomotives of Great Eastern expresses which then had running powers into this terminus, offset the immaculate Midland red. The 1914 war delayed plans for the absorption of the Lancashire & Yorkshire Railway into the London & North Western. The amalgamation did not become an accomplished fact until, ironically, a year or so before the 'groupings' of 1923. Earlier, however, the LNWR had established a 'protectorate' over the North London Railway, and the experiment was tried of running two-hour expresses between Broad Street and Birmingham.

But all this, in our context, is looking ahead. My earlier memories are, among other things, of hoardings that blazoned posters announcing competitive time-cuts by rival railways connecting important centres, while my father, a business man in Leicester, would tell me how representatives of each of the four railways serving that town called and solicited his custom. The LNWR and GNR representatives, promising speedy delivery, were undeterred by the fact that their respective trains reached Leicester only by branch lines.

By the time I was in my late-middle teens, a certain

softening of competition had been made legally possible. Inter-availability of tickets was granted between places served by two or more railways. Thus, the passenger from London to Birmingham could start from Euston and return to Paddington. 'Pooling arrangements' extended to road delivery. In Leicester, as elsewhere, the MR and LNWR clubbed together, as did the GCR and GNR. Previously each of these companies had had not merely its own design of drays and vans but its equally distinctive horses. Lovely creatures as they all were, you could never mistake a Great Northern horse, 'heavy' or light', for a Midland one.

I regarded even this small measure of railway co-operation as robbing our streets of some of their former glory, which, however, remained unimpaired on the actual railways themselves. It was as a pageant of colour that they first fascinated me, and they are a constant joy in recollection. 'Bliss was it then to be alive' if you were a railway-minded youngster, untroubled by thoughts of wasteful competition or (as yet) by a social conscience. Then, of course, railway travel was the more exciting because, let me reiterate, it was the *only* means by which one could enter a wider world.

For mechanics I had never had any taste. Liking to see the wheels go round, I could not have cared less what made them do so. Gradually, however, I became seriously interested in railway organisation, while, a little later still, I loved railways for yet another reason. A long journey by train brought, as nothing else could, a feeling of detachment, inducing reflection and setting imagination free.

'Herein,' said Robert Louis Stevenson, 'is the chief attraction of railway travel. The speed is so easy, and the train disturbs so little the scenes through which it takes us, that our hearts become full of the placidity and stillness of the country; and while the body is carried forward in the flying chain of carriages, the thoughts alight, as the humour moves them, at unfrequented stations; they make us haste up the poplar avenue that leads towards the town; they are left behind with the signalman as, shading his eyes with his hand, he watches the long train sweep away into the golden distance.'

Stevenson's is not an isolated voice. True as it may be, in the words of John Bright, that 'railways have rendered more services, and have received less thanks, than any other institution in the world', there *have* been a few discriminating appreciators not only of their practical but their less tangible benefits. 'Never let me hear you say that the railways spoil a countryside; they do, it is true, spoil this or that particular place—as, for example, Crewe, Brighton, Stratford-on-Avon—but for this disadvantage they give us I know not how many delights.' Thus Hilaire Belloc, who, having enumerated some of those delights, continued: 'The railway gives you seclusion. If you are in an express alone you are in the only spot in Western Europe where you can be certain of two or three hours to yourself. At home in the dead of night you may be awakened by a policeman or a sleepwalker or a dog. The heaths are populous. You cannot climb to the very top of Helvellyn to read your own poetry to yourself without fear of a tourist. But in the corner of a third-class going north or west you can be sure of your own company; the best, the most sympathetic, the most brilliant in the world.'

That was written in 1908. The thought of railway travel offering seclusion may now seem a little odd to some people; but such seclusion was normally to be enjoyed. 'Normally' is the operative word, to which I will presently return. Excursion trains, of which there were plenty, might be comfortably —seldom uncomfortably—filled; but, travelling by ordinary train, one was surprised and slightly resentful if a corner-seat was not available. Often one had a compartment to oneself. On some lines—if, say, one was going from St Pancras to Leicester or even to Sheffield—one could take a seat in the dining-car and retain it throughout the journey; and on the better lines the dinner, at 6s or 7s 6d, was a six-course affair, with starched napkins and all the other 'refinements' one would expect in a good hotel.

True, I am here speaking of what I personally experienced only when the new century had well set in. I imagine that while I was still a child, dining-cars, at any rate on most of the lines which ran them at all, were first class only. Yet for several years after third-class diners were available, only the really 'upper' few felt at home in them. Families like my own could have afforded to patronise them, but middle-class social custom still held us back. When we went on holiday we took sandwiches, which could usually be eaten in privacy.

I am not suggesting that today one cannot often find room and to spare in trains. Some may be virtually empty. But you cannot *count* on a restful journey, especially if you have to travel at rush hours or 'peak' periods. Things were different years ago. The thought that, even during August or on Christmas Eve, a train might be crowded never occurred to us, and much as I travelled during my late teens and in my 20s it was not until 1927 that I first stood—at Waterloo for a Bournemouth express—in a platform queue. At the time this seemed an isolated or 'freak' incident. So little in my mind did it reflect changing conditions that a year later, when my wife and I travelled from Hythe in Kent to Minehead for our honeymoon, in the height of the summer holiday season, there seemed no reason to give any forethought to the journey. Nor did we encounter real difficulty, even though delay on the Southern or in crossing London—I now forget which, so had better not cast aspersions!—caused us to reach Paddington with only a few minutes in hand. A friendly and efficient porter immediately took charge of us; but we were surprised when he had to rush us to the front of a very long train and when he secured the only two remaining seats—facing each other, but not directly—as the guard blew his whistle. No longer, it now became clear, was railway travel what it used to be!

It is surprising, indeed, that certain nineteenth-century influences had survived the first world war and had revived to some extent after it. Change was on its way in 1914, and the

16

war accelerated it, but not so dramatically as did, in its turn, the second war. Still, many of us, when the earlier 'Armageddon' broke out, felt correctly that it doomed, if it did not actually end, an epoch. Like other people who remember 1914, I have a host of poignant recollections. Yet small things have a trick of remaining, as symbols, in the imagination; and, for me, two incidents are tied up with railways.

On Friday 31 July 1914, I, then 23 and working in a publisher's office in London, was going home for the Bank Holiday weekend. There was still hope that war might be avoided—but not much; and I had at least an inkling of what war would mean if it came. The familiar, secure, comfortable, dignified order, of which for me the Midland Railway had always subconsciously been the symbol, might not only be interrupted; it might never return. I decided to make the most of what would perhaps be my last journey under accustomed conditions. Travelling by an early-evening train, I bought—a thing I had never done before, except on suburban routes—a first-class ticket. My dining compartment was almost empty, and, though the staff must have been as worried about events as I was, nothing in their demeanour betrayed the fact: dinner was served with normally quiet ceremony. As I ate, I gazed out, as I had done dozens of times before, on the passing landscape, tranquil and mellowing to harvest in the golden twilight. How I had loved that landscape, homely as it was! Now, in words John Masefield was soon to write, it became 'inestimably dear'. That journey has never faded from mind.

Nor has its sequel. When I stood on Leicester station for the return journey the following Tuesday morning, war had been declared. There was, however, no sign of anything unusual. A number of other passengers were waiting on platform three the arrival of the St Pancras train from Bradford. Then suddenly from platform four—the other side of an 'island', reserved for Midland locals and the LNW trains to Nuneaton —there came the sounds of singing and shouting. Going to discover what was happening, I beheld a revolutionary sight. A troop-train, more crowded than any train I had ever seen, had just drawn in; and—I blinked incredulous eyes—it was hauled by a North Eastern locomotive—a lovely green thing with its characteristically large, side-windowed cab, yet a shameless intruder: a 'foreigner', straying a hundred miles from home! My eyes, I thought, must be deceiving me; for, while the coaches of one company regularly worked through to other companies' systems, engines were sacrosanct. Like certain fabled monarchs, they never left their own terrain.

Verily, an age seemed to have ended. As further experience was soon to prove, it had at least come to a halt. Not—for some of us—quite immediately. Returning to platform three, I found all was still peace and decorum. The St Pancras express —'London only'—arrived dead on time and was given priority of departure over the troop-train. The journey was made with the usual punctuality and ease; but, before many weeks had' passed, travelling on the Midland, or on any other line, was— for the 'duration' and some while after—a very different matter.

Again I have digressed. To get the pre-1914 picture clear, we must remember that if the more prosperous railways paid good dividends—a schoolmaster, about 1902, told us that when we grew up we should invest what money we might have in LNWR shares—it was not only because of low costs and wages and long working hours, but because all the country's freight was still carried by rail. Income from goods traffic enabled railways to cater generously for passengers, and competition set the pace. I have no statistics, but I imagine that passengers were fewer than they are now. Many people could not afford to travel, though the major fact may be that in no case would they have thought of leaving home. The itch for moving about had not yet developed. Working-class 'commuters'—the word would have puzzled them—had to be carried, and they were encouraged to travel at unearthly hours of the morning in special workmen's trains at reduced fares.

As for holidays, comparatively few workers took them, and those who did depended mainly on excursion trains, sometimes ignominiously drawn by goods-engines. Such trains remained non-corridor long after corridors became common on ordinary trains. Most of the best expresses in the earliest years I can recall lacked corridors, while lavatory-compartments, much sought after, were still a luxury.

In proportion, however, to the stage of railway evolution, passengers—provided they were upper or middle class—were, in the main, well catered for. No doubt the social order, which railways necessarily reflected, was sadly wrong, and I awoke to this fact long before it was forced upon me, much as I continued to enjoy the benefits available only to the privileged or semi-privileged. But that is another matter. I am here concerned with railways as they were, and the picture I draw has no element of exaggeration.

Some may find this hard to believe. For instance, the young mother, looking in vain for a porter to help her with children and luggage, may not easily visualise the time when porters by the dozen were available at big stations and were never lacking at minor ones. Not, of course, that porters are now extinct, or fail sometimes to appear in reasonable numbers. But they are much less conspicuously a part of the railway scene than formerly, and there is not the old dependence on being able to obtain their services. Older readers will remember the days when, on the arrival of an express at a terminus, porters were lined up, in twos or threes, along the whole length of the platform, and when the real difficulty was to decide which of several competitors was legitimately first in the field. Many porters would greet even the morning rush-hour trains at Liverpool Street or London Bridge, when there would be few, if any, passengers with luggage—and tips. But newspapers could be picked up, and, anyway, it was part of routine, then strictly enforced, that all carriage windows had to be closed before the train was drawn back out of the station.

Only occasionally would porters be temporarily overtaxed,

as on the arrival at Torquay of the fashionable noon train from Paddington. Then the available force would hurry to empty the luggage vans, until the platform was stacked mountain-high with trunks and cases, which it took some little time, after the train had resumed its progress to Paignton and Kingswear, for the alighted passengers to identify. Few of them, though, would be irked by such delay. There was a ritualistic feeling about railway travel before the motor-car, into which all kinds of bundles and parcels can be thrown helter-skelter at the last moment, became a serious rival. The motor-car has become the symbol of hurry in a manner railways never were. Speed *during* a railway journey was expected and enjoyed; but so also, by most passengers, was the leisurely and decorous procedure at the beginning and end. I recall the Torquay scene above described as late as 1928. 'Travelling light' had not yet become the order of the day, any more than had travelling impatiently. Victorianism was not quite dead.

Victorian, both in its strength and weakness, our railway system certainly was. Planning and building were on such an ample and solid scale that much has usefully survived. Much, on the other hand, has proved an embarrassment and a burden; much that has already vanished—such as the provision on many stations of separate waiting-rooms, first-class, second-class and third-class, for men and women—now seems positively absurd.

The early railway engineers were not only superb craftsmen; their optimism made them far-sighted. They had justifiable confidence in the growth of railways, and they wisely built not merely for the moment. Yet there is a difference between the moment and eternity, and, inasmuch as railways were visualised as developing indefinitely along foreseeable paths and by foreseeable methods, their constructors lacked deeper prophetic vision. A less intrinsically sound set-up would have proved more easily adaptable to the changes, some of them naturally undreamt of, that were to come. If in certain respects their Victorian origin has served our railways

20

well, there were incubi which they were too slow in casting off, just as they were too tardy, when conditions began more radically to change, in reading the writing upon the wall. But that is my son's province.

He opened his eyes on a very different scene. Much water (and blood) had flowed under the bridges, countless thousands of trains (steam or electric) had passed through or over the bridges, since I was a child. The motor and the social revolutions were now well under way; aeroplanes droned, menacingly, in the sky. Railways, nevertheless, commanded the concentrated zeal of the small boy, and this served to revive what for some years had been my own waning enthusiasm. With the amalgamations of the many old companies into four groups, railways for me had lost much of their former appeal.

However, by merciful Providence, the young don't miss what they have never known, and, with four railways in the field, there was still enough vivid contrast to kindle partisanship for one's own chosen line. In 1936, when David was seven, the model railway which figures in this volume was tentatively started. Within a few years, as the Paddington to Seagood Railway, it attracted public attention—to such an extent that during the second war it brought food parcels from folk unknown to us in many parts of the world. Publicity was utterly alien to my intention. As a professional author, with no great inventive turn, I have found it easiest to write about matters close at hand, paradoxically forgetting that newspaper articles or books actually have the readers one subconsciously desires! This may sound silly, but it is true.

Selecting passages from my book *Paddington to Seagood,* I have included a description, with diagram, of the final layout in our South Devon home. This layout, whatever its defects or limitations in other respects, was a complete railway system in microcosm, and, though our many visitors included real railwaymen and some high railway officials, I pride myself that no fault was ever found with the strictly scientific planning, from which the elements of sound railway operation could be learned. David learned them to such good effect that, by his middle teens, he could safely and smoothly run a number of trains simultaneously—sometimes, to prove it possible, in the dark.

His interest in railways, technical, economic and social, steadily outstripped mine. While retaining an æsthetic and emotional love of the old order, he was quick to appreciate the necessity of change, however critical sometimes of the forms it took. When he started his journalistic career his specialised railway knowledge was soon turned to account, and, since railways can no longer be viewed in isolation, his interest in other forms of transport has correspondingly grown.

So much by way of enabling the reader to see the following pages in perspective. They must now be left, as best or worst they may, to speak for themselves. One final word. My own contributions are now so dated—therein lies whatever virtue they may possess—that I have smiled while disinterring them. Some of my prophecies have proved wrong. Diesel engines— little as they deserve them!—have, contrary to my expectation, been given names. Still, I complacently award myself a good mark for having awakened before 1930 to the possibility, remote as it then seemed, that the motor-car might ultimately spell the doom of railway branch lines.

HOW IT BEGAN

To begin at the beginning, I owe much to the fact that I
came intimately into contact with railways in my very early
years. Until I was five I lived in a square in the heart of
Leicester. Late in the last century the custom had not completely died out by which middle-class families dwelt over the
business premises. The distinctive vans and drays of three
railway companies—the Great Central had yet to add a fourth
—formed much of the traffic upon which I gazed through the
nursery-window, and sometimes one of the vehicles drew up
to unload its bales at our door.

Then, just round the corner, were the Midland Railway
stables, where dozens of horses were kept, and where harness-
ing or unharnessing could often be seen in progress; and

nearby lay some sidings of the railway itself, with a single wooden platform. This had once been part of the passenger terminus, then recently replaced, some little distance away, by the fine modern through station. But the old platform was still used for parcels and milk traffic; while the adjoining tracks, each with its buffers near the roadway entrance to the yard, accommodated spare passenger coaches, which were sometimes being marshalled by a shunting engine. Whenever I looked in through the white gates, within a stone's throw of my home, there was something to make me 'stand and stare'.

Another two minutes' walk, up a slope rising above a narrow cobbled street lined with warehouses, brought me to a bridge which spanned the main Midland line to the north of the new passenger station. The bridge itself, being of tubular design, precluded any sight of track or trains; but, at the far end, a flagged footpath, offering pedestrians a short cut to another part of the town, turned at right angles from the main thoroughfare and ran parallel with the railway below. Through protective wire-netting the whole busy junction was visible, with the goods station and warehouse in the near distance. There was much through traffic, including an almost constant procession of long coal trains or returning empties. Then there was the incessant local shunting, and I can hear again now the peculiar squeak of the locomotives as they rounded the curves of Engine Shed Sidings immediately below my point of vantage.

When we left the town for an inner suburb, and now that I was old enough to take my walks unaccompanied, the Midland—or London Road—passenger station, to which we were still quite near, became my favourite resort. The Great Northern Railway, which took us to the Lincolnshire coast, had its own station in Leicester. Though it served only single-track branches connecting with Peterborough and Grantham, it was, in the spacious Victorian style, an imposing terminal structure. But it lay in a remote and then slummy part of the town, which, being out of bounds, was only seldom visited by

DOUBLE HEADED: MIDLAND. Top: *Two class 2 4—4—0s approaching Armathwaite on an up train.* Bottom: *Branch opening in Northamptonshire. Midland Railway 0—4—4 No. 2022 piloting 0—6—0 No. 212 on inaugural passenger train at Higham Ferrers on 1 May 1894 on the branch from Wellingborough*

DOUBLE HEADED: WEST COUNTRY. Top: *Western Region 6931 and 7820 climbing long bank from Bodmin Road to Doublebois on 15-coach summer Saturday Newquay—Paddington train in 1959.* Middle: *As many will remember the Western Region in pre-diesel days. The 'Cornish Riviera Express' on Blachford viaduct near Cornwood in 1957.* Bottom: *Unusual combination. Nos. 9023 and 5148 on 1955 summer Saturday Manchester—Penzance express leaving Newton Abbot*

DOUBLE HEADED: SCOTLAND. Top: *Unusual combination descending the 1 in 50 bank into Oban with half-day excursion in August 1937. Locomotives 17604 (Caledonian 3F) and 14691 'Brodic Castle'.* Bottom: *'Scottish Rambler' with restored* HR *No. 103 and* GNSR *No. 49 at Stranraer Junction on 15 April 1963*

DOUBLE HEADED: NARROW GAUGE. Top: *Port Erin boat train, Isle of Man Railway, August 1961. No. 16 piloting No. 10.* Middle: *Study in steam at Festiniog.* Bottom: *'Sans Pareil' piloting 'Sir Aubrey Brocklebank' on a Ravenglass-bound train at Irton Road on Ravenglass & Eskdale Railway in 1925*

me. Of real antiquarian interest was the West Bridge terminus of the Midland, then (and long afterwards) still used by a few locals. Its quaintly primitive single platform had served the Leicester & Swannington Railway in 1830. (Unfortunately it is apocryphal that an accident on this line led to the invention of the locomotive whistle.) Early in the present century came the Great Central on its high viaduct through Leicester, where it displaced some Roman remains. How thrilled I was to see the new railway under construction, and when at last it was finished and I came to travel on it, how strangely quiet seemed its atmosphere, accentuated by the muffled whistle of its green locomotives!

But, because it was handier and busier, the main Midland station—shared, modestly in numbers if aggressively in spirit, by the North Western trains—remained my normal haunt. Platform tickets, levying their heavy and sometimes prohibitive toll upon youngsters, had not yet come generally into vogue, and as London Road was an 'open' station, one could, with intent to loiter, wander about it unmolested. Leicester, most spick and span of industrial cities, is still proud of her principal station, with its yellow-tiled cleanliness and brightness. There was reason for special pride 40 or so years ago, when, being of recent construction, it contrasted more vividly than now with other stations.

Designed on generous yet simple lines, with its four long platforms (two islands) entirely under cover, it had its own unobtrusive orderliness, and preserved, even at its busiest moments, some spirit of calm. Only when the little LNWR tank engines arrived or were preparing to depart with their Nuneaton branch-line trains, which took us on the first stage of our journey when we went on holiday to North Wales, was its atmosphere temporarily agitated. In the matter of noise the locomotives of the different railways, in that pre-grouping era, varied considerably; and the North Western were sinners above the rest. You could never mistake the sound of escaping steam from their safety-valves, and their whistle, which, contrary to Midland practice, they emitted on every possible occasion, was excessively shrill. I liked the black-and-white coaches of the North Western—'purple-brown and spilt-milk' was, I believe, the official formula; but to me, for whom noise has always been a synonym for hell, that whistle made travel on 'The Premier Line' a nightmare.

Even so, I sometimes lamented that the North Western had only small running powers into Leicester. As I came to have wider experience, I deplored the lack of variety at London Road. One express daily, in each direction, carried a through Lancashire & Yorkshire coach, with its black and deep-orange livery; while, during the summer months, a Midland & Great Northern Joint line engine, khaki in colour, might be seen heading a train for Cromer, Yarmouth and Lowestoft. For the rest, everything was just MR; and though I gratefully recognised that the Midland locomotives were relatively quiet in their habits, and though I could appreciate their neat design and well-groomed appearance, yet somehow, efficient as they were, they *looked* less powerful than the engines of other companies. Moreover, they were painted monotonously red —a beautiful red, I had to admit—to match the fine clerestory coaches, then the last word in comfort, and they were merely numbered, with the arbitrary exception of one locomotive called *Princess of Wales*.

Yet, with all its limitations, London Road was not to be despised. On the highway from the metropolis to the north, it was also an important link between the eastern and western counties, with branches radiating to Birmingham, Rugby, Peterborough, Nottingham, and elsewhere. I had the time-table by heart, and can feel again my emotion as the hour approached for the arrival of the 10.20 'up' from Bradford to London or the 11.30 'down' Scottish express. This latter, composed of two portions to be divided at Carlisle, was of joint-line stock—in Midland colours, but bearing (on the forward coaches) the lettering M. and N.B., and (on the rearward carriages) M. and G.S.W. Shortly before the great moment the signalman in his box halfway along the platform struck three resounding blows on his gong. Then the signal-arm near the cabin dropped with a thud. A spirit of expectancy filled the air; newsboys and buffet-boys appeared with their baskets; porters came leaping across the tracks; a postman arrived with the mails; the assistant stationmaster, alert yet kindly, emerged from his office; and at last, with a motion magnificently graceful, the train glided in.

For five minutes, whilst the engine was being uncoupled and a fresh one (boisterous, by Midland standards, with excess of energy) was being attached; while passengers were scurrying nervously hither and thither, and trunks and boxes were being trundled about pell-mell, I revelled in the bustle. As I scanned the destination-boards on the trains, my spirit took wings. To read *Liverpool (Central)* or *Leeds* on a carriage was, at a fairly early age, to be transported to places already known. *Edinburgh (Waverley)*, *Aberdeen (via Forth Bridge)*, or *Glasgow (St Enoch)* stirred dreams later to be fulfilled. But, of all the legends, *London (St Pancras)* was, at that time, the most alluring; and I marvelled at the phlegm of the ordinary passenger. There, in a corner of that first-class compartment, sat a man who would perhaps, within a few short hours, be treading the magic pavements of Cornhill or Fleet Street, or watching the ships pass through the open jaws of the Tower Bridge. Yet he was doggedly frowning over his newspaper, apparently heedless. If only I were in his place!

As soon as the train, drawn by one of Johnson's famous single-drivers, had left for London, Manchester or Scotland, the indicator on the platform was changed, as the case might be, to *All Stations to Burton-on-Trent* or *All Stations to Derby*. These, indeed, were but two among the many possible 'pointers'; for upon Leicester, as I have said, branches from every direction converged. When no expresses were to be seen, there were the locals; and, humble as these might appear by contrast, even they were invested with romance. For there were then few long-distance cross-country expresses in

England as a whole, and, until the Great Central line was opened, none of these passed through Leicester. By the Midland route we could travel quickly to 'Town' or to the north; but to go east or west involved starting in the All Stations to Peterborough, or the Hinkley and All Stations to Birmingham train. (The reason why the Midland slows to Birmingham did not stop until they reached Hinckley was that, as far as that town, they ran over the metals of the North Western line to Nuneaton.)

The locals were to me, therefore, the first links in a long chain of adventure. . . . Leicester might have the disadvantage of being 'inland far'; but its central position offered at least one compensation . . . my knowledge of England, and my first-hand acquaintance with its railways, became extensive. To such a degree did two enthusiasms coincide that a special affection or distaste for a particular district helped—sometimes unfairly—to determine my regard for the railway serving it, and *vice-versa*. Thus, when I went to boarding-school at Cambridge, where for nights I lay miserably awake listening to the shunting of a 'foreign' company's trains, I acquired such a dislike of the Great Eastern Railway that, for long afterwards in London, I could never hear the husky whistle of a certain type of GE engine without experiencing again a queer feeling in the pit of the stomach. Only when I was much older, and came to love East Anglia (now better known) for its own sake, did my emotional attitude to the GER undergo a corresponding change. I say my 'emotional' attitude because, by purely railway standards, none would have ranked the Great Eastern very high. Yet its leisurely methods and primitive rolling-stock were pleasantly in keeping with the tranquil, unsophisticated countryside through which it passed. . . .

It was, again, as a boy, loitering about the London Road station at Leicester, that I first gained some insight into the complexity of railway operation, and observed clue after clue that enabled me dimly to visualise the system as a marvellously integrated whole. At first the network of lines and array of signals looked as though they might have been deliberately designed to impress the eye of youth. Stage by stage, however, I came to realise that there was not a point, not a cross-over, not a siding, not a signal but had its specific justification, and that, so far from the planners having tried to make the layout as complicated as possible, they had, by the most careful pre-vision, the most expert skill and the most minute attention to the requirements of the traffic at this particular station, sim-plified it to the utmost practicable degree, so that, nothing essential being lacking but nothing superadded, all the neces-sary movements of trains could be carried out expeditiously and without a hitch.

(Pictures page 38)

THE AGE OF TOYS

Model railways of a kind are almost as old as railways themselves. 'Angry models jetted steam' and 'a pretty railway' ran in the garden described in Tennyson's *The Princess* (1847).

Scale-model railways are just as old as our century; but for some years after an enterprising young man called Bassett-Lowke had built a passable miniature representation of the LNWR locomotive *Black Prince,* and had thus laid the foundations of the famous firm bearing his name, models not only remained crude by the standards of today but were few in number and correspondingly expensive. One had, therefore, to be satisfied with *toys*; and primitive in the extreme most of them were. Perhaps, while one was still very young, that was all to the good. Make-believe, not scientific realism, is the proper pabulum for small people; and though I cannot recall the time when playing at trains was not my favourite pursuit, I was never in my earliest years at a loss for raw material.

Even in chapel, to which I was taken every Sunday, I found that an excellent game of trains could be enjoyed by pushing hymn-books along the book-ledge. True, progress was sometimes slow, for my father's eyes were the signals, and only when they were turned away from me could they be deemed, in railway parlance, to be 'off'. Still, if under difficulties, my 'trains' continued to run. When, however, a boy reaches the age of eight or nine, it is natural and right that scientific interest should begin to come into play, and that toys should bear at least some likeness to the things they purport to represent. In those days, unfortunately, when one had outgrown the clumsy wooden engines of infancy, and had exhausted the resources of private invention, there was no satisfactory substitute. My parents took great pains in choosing toys, but they could not buy what was not on the market, and I remember vividly my disappointment when, one Christmas morning, I opened the first 'real' train and lines I had been promised.

The steam-driven 'engine'—save the mark!—was a hideous contraption on four wheels. Its boiler was of brass, naked and unashamed; its chimney and safety-valve were utter caricatures; and its whistle, realistic and exciting a feature as it might be in one sense, was about 20 times scale size. The tender and the three passenger coaches were also, of course, four-wheelers; and not only did they lack every other kind of realism, but each vehicle was painted a different colour. The 'track' was a small circle of tin rails.

A few evenings later, the train having in the meantime made many hundred of convolutions under hand power, everything was set for the trial run by steam. Nervous and agitated were we all, as the ugly container under the cab of the locomotive was filled with evil-smelling methylated-spirit and the wick lighted. The whistle was placed at 'open', and in due course, after what seemed an interminable wait, its shrill sound proclaimed that steam was 'up'. I will draw a veil over the ensuing scene. Suffice it that the engine's antics were weird and alarming in the extreme, and that, as it lacked governors or controls, and as we were all too scared to touch it, as alternately it raced or ambled round the track, still emitting its now monotonous whistle and (to my mother's horror) bespattering the green tablecloth, we were relieved when at last it turned over on its side, and, though it seemed likely to burst at any moment, was heroically carried by my father to a place where its exuberance might safely be allowed to cool. . . .

Then, a year or two later, I beheld in a shop window a vision that quickened my pulse. There, positively, were exhibited some miniature clockwork locomotives and some passenger coaches immediately recognisable as such. They would seem poor enough today even as toys. They were evidence, none the less, if I did not grasp their full significance at the time, that the age of models was dawning. Not only did those engines and carriages, four-wheelers though they were, possess certain clear resemblances to real trains: they were actually painted and lettered in semi-correct LNWR and Midland style. Moreover, they were relatively cheap. . . . Soon it was possible to buy coal wagons having some similitude to their prototypes, and to replace signals of Continental style by ones of English pattern. But by this time my ardour was somewhat abating, owing to the tedium in setting out and afterwards packing up the railway whenever I used it; and all occupations of my own choice were brought to an end when in 1906 I started at boarding-school. . . .

When at last I took up the hobby of model railways, I was amazed to discover how many people of very different types, including friends whom I had known for a long time, but between whom and myself our common interest had remained a secret, were railway-lovers. That absurd fear of seeming childish had sealed their lips—and mine. But for my own silence, I might have enjoyed much more 'railway' companionship than I did during the quarter-century after I left school. What astonishes me in retrospect, however, is that through all those years I remained comparatively ignorant of the developments in the hobby and of its popularity among the 'young of all ages'.

This is the more remarkable because as long ago as 1921, when his attention had been arrested by a newspaper article

GREAT CENTRAL. Top: *In common with the other important stations on 'the last main line', Leicester Central consisted of an island platform with bays at each end for local trains. The northern end is shown nearing completion.* Bottom: *The new line was enthusiastically welcomed by farmers*

LEICESTER LONDON ROAD. Top: *Exterior at the turn of the century.* Bottom: *Mid-morning lull showing the full length of the two island platforms*

of mine, with its quite incidental reference to 'a certain toy-shop in Holborn, where railway models are exhibited', I had made the acquaintance, which soon ripened into friendship, of Mr W. J. Bassett-Lowke, who may, I suppose, be called the true father of model railways. I remember that we visited together the Wembley Exhibition of 1924. Having examined and stepped on to the footplate of the GWR locomotive *Caerphilly Castle*—first of a noble class—and of its equally new LNER rival, we lunched on Union fare in the dining-car of the South African Railways, and, while appreciating the generally high standard of efficiency and comfort, reflected on the lack of foresight that had fixed the gauge at 3 ft 6 in. Yet we discovered so many other common tastes that railways and models were seldom discussed. And though I sometimes looked in at the Holborn premises, I still retained the impression—betrayed by that inept allusion to a 'toy-shop'—that Messrs Bassett-Lowke catered largely for the better-class juvenile market. I knew, of course, that they made expensive advertisements for the railway and shipping companies, as also for private scientific connoisseurs and for a few mature enthusiasts who had the courage to run their own model systems. But I imagined that these last, so boldly risking the superior smile of their friends, were in a very small minority. Even so, having myself now grown a tougher skin, I inwardly vowed that I would join their numbers if opportunity ever occurred.

SIX CHANGES

As children, my sisters and I were taken annually by my father from our home in Leicester to visit his parents at Redbrook-on-Wye. Getting from Leicester to Redbrook was, in those days, at the turn of the century, an exciting if leisurely affair. That journey, occupying less than four hours, is now made as far as Chepstow in a through express linking New-castle-upon-Tyne with South Wales. Forty years ago it filled the day and necessitated six changes. It began in a Midland train that stopped at all stations to Birmingham, excluding those owned by a 'foreign' company over whose metals part of this route lay. I could tell when our mere running-powers ended and we rejoined our own Midland line by the change back from one type of signal-arm to another.

New Street station at Birmingham, shared by London &
North Western and Midland trains, seemed so vast and noisy
that pleasure was temporarily turned to dread. It had for me,
perhaps because of the tunnels by which it was approached
and left, a slightly sinister atmosphere, emphasised by the
excessively shrill locomotive blasts from the North Western
platforms and by the weird blowing of horns that here formed
part of that company's signalling arrangements. I was glad
that we kept safely to the Midland side, and was relieved
when we were seated in the North of England to Bristol
express, which, with its spacious clerestory coaches, took us on
our next lap.

At the top of the Lickey incline there was a moment's
compulsory stop, and the descent to Bromsgrove made me
hold my breath, save when, peering through the window, I
was diverted from thought of danger by the spectacle of a
train climbing in the opposite direction, with the special
banking engine puffing energetically in the rear. At Worcester
(Shrub Hill) we alighted; and though, in its chocolate-and-
cream livery, the Great Western train was already standing,
engineless, in the bay, we had an hour to wait for its departure. In contrast to my mother, who chose to arrive at a
station only at the last moment, my father liked to 'take time
by the forelock'. But this seemed an ample enough margin
even for him. So, as we had eaten our sandwiches and fruit,
we filed out into Worcester to see the Cathedral and the river.

The rest of the journey lay over Great Western territory;
and while for other reasons my affection for the GWR is still so
lively that it gives me immense satisfaction to be living now
on its main line to Cornwall, my love for it was born of those
travels to Monmouthshire. The romantic scenery through
which it passed added to its own spell; the romance of the
railway in turn invested the landscape with greater charm. So
far from spoiling the country, except at certain points, a railway for me gives it the final perfection. The fact that the
Great Western track ran sheer alongside the sinuous Wye,

and that the quiet single line crossed from the far to the near bank of the river within sight of my grandparents' window, completed my happiness in the scene.

On leaving Worcester (for I have anticipated) we were all agog for our first glimpse of the Malvern Hills. From Malvern to Hereford, past timbered villages, orchards and hop-fields, we travelled in the express from London. The green engine with its brightly gleaming brasswork, its distinctive panting rhythm, and its *name*—it was probably one of the superb *Achilles* single-drivers—seemed much more impressive than did the neat, but merely numbered and somehow more ordinary, Midland locomotives. From Hereford to Ross, bridging again and again the middle Wye, here flowing through fine open country with lush meadows and red and white cattle, and then in two more stages through the dramatically contrasted deep valley of the lower river, we progressed slowly once more in locals drawn by little fat pannier tanks. At Symonds Yat, where the single track opened into a loop, we had to wait for the train in the opposite direction, and thus had opportunity to drink in the full majesty of the gorge in the gathering spring or autumn twilight. At Monmouth (Troy) we made our final change—having two miles to go in the Chepstow train. On our return journey we had an additional change—making seven in all—at Worcester (Forgate Street), from which a single-coach 'train' took us to Shrub Hill.

THE LAST MAIN LINE

As if it were not good fortune enough to live in a town served by three railways, I had the thrill as a child of seeing a fourth come to Leicester. It was soon to be called the Great Central, but during the earlier stages of construction it was known as 'The London Extension' of the Manchester, Sheffield & Lincolnshire Railway. Engineering works on this vast scale were quite new to all but elderly folk with long memories. In any case methods of railway building had advanced since everything depended upon the brawn of navvies; excavating and other machines added to the novelty. At Leicester, as elsewhere, the young—and not so young—gaped with fascination at these latest wonders of the nineteenth century, now nearing its end. Ironically, despite the Midland Railway's understandable hostility to its coming rival, material for the Great Central, including girders for bridges, was carried in Midland trains and then delivered to the site on Midland horse-drays. No other method of transport was then possible.

The new line was fully opened for traffic in 1899. I first travelled on it from Leicester to Ashby Magna, which gave us nearer access than the Midland station at Countesthorpe to the hamlet where my grandfather lived—or had lived. On this occasion I was, in fact, attending his funeral; but melancholy was offset by the excitement of going by the Great Central, which passed through—or over—our town on a viaduct.

What an impression the Leicester Central Station made on a nine-year-old! Whereas we had to descend from ground level to reach the trains at the Midland Station, with its two island platforms entirely under cover, we climbed steeply *upstairs* at the Central, which consisted of one very long island, with bays at both ends, and was only partly sheltered by an awning. Added to the sheer newness and cleanliness, there was a sense of height, space and air. The green Pollitt engines had, even in that era of lovely locomotives, their own distinctive appeal, while the two-colour paintwork of the coaches resembled without imitating the Great Western livery. (Later it was abandoned for plain teak.) Another novelty was the muffled whistle of the GC engines, so different from the full, business-like tone of the Midland or the uninhibited screech of the LNW.

Ashby Magna, in its rustic setting, also proved to be an island station. Island stations were, indeed, standard practice on the Great Central, and one marvels why it was left for the promoters of the last main line to discover the simple fact that two running tracks didn't demand separately constructed platforms and buildings for up and down traffic. One thing and another combined to make early travel on the GCR not merely an adventure but an inherently 'different' experience. Somehow, for me, the Great Central had a dreamlike quality. It did not seem quite of this bustling world. For one thing, 'The London Extension' had very few branches. At Leicester the only local trains were stopping main-line ones, so that the volume of traffic was never great. Then, between Leicester and the new terminus at Marylebone—small, clean and bright, with ferns in the circulating area—the route was more rural and (through the Chiltern country) more picturesque than the Midland.

Still, for all its air of quiet detachment, the Great Central made its mark. Its coal and mineral trains relieved the growing congestion on other systems; and though its passengers had for the most part to be lured from those same rivals, since itself touched no town of any size that was not already served by one or more of the older companies, it added a few small towns and many villages to the railway map. It was particularly welcomed in some districts by farmers and dairy-farmers who, in these pre-petrol days, had been too far from a station to send their produce by rail.

Between big industrial centres the GCR prompted new speed contests. Typical was the competition between it and the Midland for the London—Leicester traffic. Repeatedly, before the 1914 war cried a halt, one or other company lopped off minutes in the journey time. Street hoardings carried large posters proclaiming the latest triumph. Then, by building a short line from Woodford Halse to Banbury, thus linking its own 'trunk' with that of the Great Western, the Great Central, with the collaboration of the NE and GW companies, inaugurated what at the time seemed those wonderful cross-country dining-car expresses connecting North East England with the South and South Wales.

This was indeed a revolutionary innovation, adding, so to

speak, a new dimension to railway travel.

Alas! it all came a little late. While the GCR, with its slogan *Forward*, was growing up, counter progress was at work. The motor revolution had begun. *Forward!* Well, perhaps so; but no longer, in a changed world, on Great Central metals.

(*Pictures page 37*)

CROSS-COUNTRY JOURNEYS

The other day* I was waiting upon the railway station at Ely when an express arriving at the opposite platform was labelled from end to end: 'Felixstowe, Ipswich and Sheffield'. On those destination-boards I read the doom of what to me is one of the pleasantest features of our English life—the cross-country journey.

In a highly-organised state like Germany the cross-country journey, as we have hitherto understood it, is unknown. In the German Republic the average rate of travel is the same between any two towns of reasonable size, no matter where they are situated. A friend of mine, an authority on such matters, once explained this to me over a luncheon table in Baden Baden. Our British railways, he conceded, ran faster trains than any which Germany could boast. But such trains were confined to certain main-line routes. If you want to go

* Written in 1926

47

from London to Birmingham, or from Bristol to Leeds, all well and good. But heaven help the man who is in a hurry to get from Stamford to Prestatyn or from Walsall to Boston.

Since that conversation several years have passed, and in the meantime efficiency has at last begun to lay its ugly hands upon our iron roads. The recent amalgamations, with their inevitable standardisation, have robbed our railways of much of their former romance and colour, and already there is rising a generation of schoolboys who have never known the chocolate-and-white coaches of the old North Western or the blue-liveried locomotives of the late-lamented Caledonian. Here in itself is matter enough for tears. But the gradual elimination of the cross-country journey is an even greater tragedy. Already little stations like that of Bury St Edmunds, which have enjoyed decades of peace, broken only by the panting of fussy 'locals', are on the highroad of the great new expresses that thunder from east to west; while giant engines, hauling luxurious trains for a stage of their through journey from the Midlands to Penzance, are now to be seen at the very shrine of Shakespeare himself. No doubt all this is to the material benefit of the business community, and there may be occasions when I myself shall be glad not to spend the best part of a day in covering 150 miles. Still, I recall the many hours of quiet happiness which, thanks to bad connections, have come to me when I have been left stranded and isolated upon the up platform of Dreamingham-on-the-Marsh or the down platform of Sleepytown-in-the-Wold.

It is true that, unless road competition succeeds some day in closing our branch railway lines, there will still be cross-country journeys in one sense. There will always be slow trains connecting the villages with the nearest market-town. But the point is that you and I, the long-distance travellers, will no longer have to use them; and great will be our loss. Instead of the ruddy farmer, who talks so knowingly about the weather and the crops and the cattle, or the old market-woman who is so eager to tell you about her rheumatism, her past life and her son in Australia, you will have the companionship of commercial travellers (of the smarter sort) or of business magnates, some of whom may be travelling without change of carriage from, say, Newcastle-upon-Tyne to Cardiff. Comfort and convenience are being increased; but variety, surprise, material and opportunity for reflection—the things that nourish and quicken the mind—are being lost through the disappearance of the cross-country journey.

It may, of course, be argued that, since slow trains must always be run for the accommodation of short-distance passengers, it is still open to the long-distance traveller to use them. There is nothing to prevent his setting out from London to Inverness in the All Stations to New Barnet train, with its City typists and bowler-hatted, pink-faced junior clerks, and proceeding thence, with frequent breaks, by means of a series of stopping locals, which would introduce him successively to Huntingdonshire and Lincolnshire farmers, Northumbrian colliers and ironworkers, and so on. There is nothing to prevent him—save those tyrants of custom, convention and inertia which forbid our doing most of the things that are best worth doing. And here I speak not as a superior, but as one under the same condemnation. For, despite my praise of the cross-country journey, I yield to none in my love of a corner-seat in an express. Much as I have enjoyed cross-country journeys, I have never set out upon one without an inward groaning at the prospect.

To begin with, the old-fashioned cross-country journey— it is still just possible to speak of it in the present—often necessitates very early rising in the morning—a thing against which the natural man in me has always rebelled. Never of my own free will should I catch a train at six o'clock if there were a possible one at ten. But, whenever I have been compelled by the exigencies of cross-country travel to be up betimes, I have never failed to be rewarded. I, too—when, but for the necessity of catching some pottering train at a wayside station, I should have been snoring between the sheets of some village inn—have gone forth alone, like Saul Kane, along the open road. I, too, like him—only without, I hope, having plumbed all his depths of depravity—have seen the station brook babbling out of paradise, and, as the sun has come up through the mist, have heard the sound of an early plough upon the hillside, and the song of the lark soaring into the smokeless heavens, and the very noise of a railway engine shunting, blended into one glorious symphony of regeneration. When, however, the work of railway organisation is complete, and the cross-country journey is a thing of the past, what shall we urban folk know of summer dawns across the fields, of little towns in their sleepy hollows, of the unsophisticated and cleansing life of the countryside? It is not that these things will cease to be. We often hear it said that there will soon be no more country left in England. It is nonsense. But increasingly it will be the fact that those who want the country will have deliberately to seek it; and a thing deliberately sought seldom brings the same satisfaction as a thing accidentally encountered.

A CORNER OF ESSEX

It was to fill in a small gap in my knowledge of Essex—a county much maligned and undervalued by people who have never visited it—that I recently* left the main-line train at Kelvedon, between Chelmsford and Colchester, and committed myself to the adventure of a journey on the Tollesbury Light Railway. Truly, one need not travel far to discover things strange and unexpected. Kelvedon is little more than an hour's run from London. Yet the tract of country that lies eastward of it is hardly surpassed for elemental peace by the remotest parts of Cornwall or Cumberland; while to find anywhere else in Europe a parallel to its primitive railway service one would probably have to go to Spain.

The Kelvedon—Tollesbury line forms an integral part of the London & North Eastern system, and the carriages, while of an unusual and tramcar design, are of standard gauge. Only the stations possess the outward picturesqueness of the toy railway. It is the functional rather than the organic eccentricities of this line that cause one to rub one's eyes and to doubt whether one is really living in the twentieth century.

The branch is just over eight miles in length, and the distance is covered (on the time-sheet) in 40 minutes. A single

* Written in 1928

train makes the return journey thrice every week-day, and rests altogether from its labours on the Sabbath. Passengers of whom there are few in this isolated and thinly-populated area, are carried in an odd coach or two appended to a string of bumping and clanging goods wagons. The line exists primarily for the jam factory that nestles amid acres of its own orchards at Tiptree, and human freight is given every possible reminder that it is of secondary importance.

When, for example, the train left Kelvedon the other morning, it consisted of two passenger coaches. With much ado, we were despatched at schedule time. But we had not gone many yards before we stopped, and backed into the sidings to pick up some trucks. There was no apparent reason why the trucks should not have been marshalled and attached beforehand. But since the whole traffic of the branch is operated by a single engine, without the assistance even of a shunting horse, the excruciating jerks and noises to which passengers are subjected are probably unavoidable. Eventually, at any rate, we got away. Within a quarter of a mile, however, we came again to a standstill, with much grinding of brakes and reverberation of buffers. Looking out of the window, my astonished eyes beheld the driver descending from his footplate to open the gates of a level crossing. Returning leisurely to his engine, he pulled the train through, and we then suffered the pangs and groans of another stoppage while the guard jumped off in the rear to close the gates.

Happily, most of the level crossings are unprotected, the engine merely giving warning of its approach by repeated whistles. At the intermediate stations—two of which rejoice in the names of Tolleshunt Knights and Tolleshunt D'Arcy—shunting operations were resumed, and at Tiptree we returned five or six times to the platform before finally leaving it. Each station consists of a short strip of pavement, with a small flowered garden and a superannuated railway carriage for the waiting-room. Since tickets are issued by the guard *en route*, no booking-offices are needed. Nor are there any signals or signalboxes. The solitary engine, fantastic as are some of its tricks, has apparently not acquired the art of running into itself.

So, in the fullness of time, we—that is to say, a commercial traveller and myself—reached Tollesbury, which, lying half a mile inland on the peninsula formed by the Blackwater estuary and another sheltered inlet of the sea, was of considerable importance in bygone days. The village takes its name from the fact that the Saxons had a station here for collecting tolls of ships entering the river. But it is now left to dream of its past, with nothing more than a little yachting, boat-repairing and fishing for its occupations. The district is rich in Roman remains.

The evening train leaves Tollesbury before seven o'clock. It was through no fear of missing this not very elusive express that I reached the station an hour earlier. The station, well removed even from such life as the village affords, seemed as excellent a place as any for rest and contemplation. Sitting solitary on the platform, I drank my fill of the broad, windswept landscape. In the foreground, mellow in the light of early evening, fields of waving wheat sloped down toward the marshes, beyond which, on the blue water of the bay, a single white sail was visible. The village of West Mercea, to the northward, presented the only sign of human habitation. For the rest, the multi-coloured fields, dappled with shadows from the swiftly-moving clouds, spread away to distant horizons. A drove of cows came down the road that intersects the station at right angles. Crossing the rails, they ambled along a leafy lane to some hidden farm. The cowman, as he passed, removed the straw from his mouth to bid me good evening. Then, once more, I was alone in the world.

Presently, however, the station awoke to life. Three impish maids of six or seven summers appeared upon the scene, and cast coquettish eyes at me as they gambolled upon the platform, which they were obviously in the habit of using as a playground. A float drove up, and two churns of milk were deposited upon the station, where there already lay some dozen baskets of fruit consigned to Stratford Market. Then sundry villagers began to arrive, and soon there was at least a dozen of them. Fear seized me that the train might be uncomfortably crowded! I had not yet realised that one of the prime functions of the station was to supply a rendezvous for local gossip. Finally the whole staff, in the person of one porter, turned up.

The train was now heard in the distance. At last the string of arks and wagons came to a spluttering standstill. A clergyman and one other person alighted, and myself and one other passenger took their places. The engine was detached, and while it performed its mystic rites, the guard and porter, voluntarily assisted by several of the spectators, unloaded a few parcels and bales, and got the milk and fruit aboard. This heavy task accomplished, they squatted on the platform for a smoke and a chat, and were joined by the driver and his mate, who had now finished their convolutions. Peace, only accentuated by the genial buzz of conversation, again settled upon the scene.

At last the guard looked at his watch, and in tones of cold indifference said: 'Well, perhaps we had better be going.' The driver and fireman mounted their engine; a shrill blast was blown upon the whistle; a chorus of good-byes from the assembled crowd embarrassed the one departing native who shared my carriage; and, with violent tuggings and gruntings, the last train of the day left Tollesbury.

BRISTOL TEMPLE MEADS. Top: *The imposing frontage at about the turn of the century.* Bottom: *On platform 9 on a summer Saturday in 1958*

THE CK & P. Top: *Diesel multiple unit near Bassenthwaite Lake in 1955.* Bottom: *Up 'Lakes Express' at Keswick, August 1960*

THE COMPANY

It was in the spring of 1936, when—having now a daughter as well as a son—we moved of necessity into a rather larger house in our Essex suburb, that I first had room for a layout. Even then I was slow to seize opportunity, though it stared me in the face. Attached to the house was a garage, not needed for a car. It measured 15 ft 6 in. by 13 ft; it was already equipped with electric lighting and gas heating; while halfway along one side of it ran a carpenter's bench. We had been in residence three months before it occurred to nimbler wits than mine that David, then nearly seven, might have this bench as permanent site for his first Hornby train and rails. He and I played for some weeks with this train and track, with its single siding, before—as much for my own satisfaction as his —I added a second junction. Later I extended this bench the whole one-way length of the garage.

It was then, if I did not realise it at the time, that my own model railway, not superseding David's but including it, germinated in my mind. The fructifying of the idea took further time; and when at last there came the vision of my own system, a psychological dragon seemed to bar the ground. That I had a small boy might have struck some people as an additional—perhaps the sole—reason for my having what I craved. To me, however, believing that expensive mechanical models are injurious to very young children, it appeared an almost insuperable obstacle. David, to be sure, was no longer an infant, and had shown that he could manage his own train with care. Nevertheless, the larger railway now taking shape in my fancy would be too much for a child of his age to use freely—let alone to possess. Would it be fair to place so much forbidden fruit within his reach? Why, on the other hand, should I forego the fulfilment of my own long-cherished dream?

Having talked things over between ourselves, we summoned David into committee. We explained the whole position to him, in the faith that children respond to reason and confidence. He readily accepted the first finding of the meeting: that he should no longer speak of his railway, but should henceforth call it ours. He quickly assimilated the idea of its belonging impersonally, like a real railway, to the 'company'. It was further settled that he should retain possession of his own engine and vehicles, allowing me the joint use of them in return for the privilege of having a free run of my projected network of brass track, which would be so strong as to be virtually foolproof. But the better locomotives and rolling-stock which I had now contemplated buying were not to be touched by him, though of course he would be able, under supervision, to share in the general fun and gradually to acquire the knowledge and sense of responsibility that would qualify him for a larger directorship in the future.

So far, so good. It is one thing for a child—as for some children of larger growth—to make an agreement: the keeping of it may be another matter. Any fears we entertained were, however, quickly allayed. So scrupulously and amicably was the contract observed from the outset that I could leave my trains in their respective sidings, knowing they would be free from interference. After three months, moreover, accidents became very rare. At first David revelled when we had a 'smash'; but before long, having a map of the system clearly in his mind and planning all movements with grave forethought, he felt it a genuine disgrace if a train were derailed through faulty point-setting, or if, beyond the degree that was inevitable on our original layout, we got our traffic into such a muddle that locomotives, coaches or wagons had ignominiously to be lifted or pushed by hand.

Alike from preference and as a prophecy and foretaste of the time when we should live upon its system, we had decided, in the slogan of those days, to 'Go Great Western'. That David raised no objection attested the degree to which we had infected him, who had as yet no first-hand knowledge of the GWR, with our own enthusiasm; for youth tends to like what is familiar, and only a few minutes' walk from our house was a fine vantage-point overlooking the main LNER line to Colchester and the East Coast. But repeated sight of *The Flushing Continental* or (in summer months) of *The Eastern Belle,* with its smart assemblage of Pullman cars, or of the goods trains to and from the Harwich ferry, bearing romantic names like Milan or Wein, never for a moment shook his loyalty—based at it was upon 'the evidence of things not seen'—to the Great Western.

Our first model railway, in that Essex garage, suffered severe teething troubles. Every possible mistake was made, but valuable experience was gained through trial and error, fun mingling with exasperation. Among red-letter days for 'the company' were those on which there arrived respectively some true scale-model Exley coaches and *King George V*, our first really worthy locomotive. From the moment *King George V* came into our possession, its prototype haunted the children's imagination like some fabled deity. One day, they told themselves, with bated breath—*one* day, if they were lucky—they might 'truly' see the real *King George*.

Before then, however, another three years were to pass, during which time there was a domestic move to a certain 'village', already a suburban outpost of London, in Hertfordshire. There, the brevity of our stay not being foreseen, we achieved a more ambitious model railway layout in two attic rooms made into one. It was now that the Paddington to Seagood Railway—David had invented the name 'Seagood' for the smaller terminus, which we pictured as being on the coast—began to attract local, then wider, attention. Hitherto I had regarded the railway-room as a sanctuary to which I could retire at will, 'the world forgetting, by the world forgot'. Now I could no longer count on being undisturbed. Visitors arrived to see the model. They were the precursors of hundreds who would eventually come, invited, self-invited or uninvited. If their visits were sometimes richly rewarding, sometimes embarrassing, they provided us all—not least the junior members of 'the board'—with a liberal education in the diversities of human nature.

RATIONALISATION

(From *The Master-Light: Letters to David*, 1932)

I have never lost my early passion for railways. My interest
in them today is many-sided, and I have just been reading a
seven-column newspaper report on the Annual General Meeting of the London, Midland & Scottish Company with as
much pleasure, of its own different kind, as in any other mood
I can read *Macbeth* or *Doctor Thorne*. Yet familiarity and a

sense of utilitarian values have not staled the thrill which the sight of a train in motion gives me, or diminished my boyish zest for studying the various types of locomotive, or debating the relative merits of different colour-schemes for rolling-stock. I know that most small boys like playing at trains; but your intensive concentration on the game suggests that you may share my own enthusiasm, and I look forward to the happy hours which you and I may spend together, when you are older, in loitering about stations, upon bridges, or in fields adjoining the iron road. But, here again, the differences in our ages will tell.

When I was young, there were 16 'grand trunk' railways in Britain, besides many lesser lines; and each company had its own distinctive engines, coaches, and other features. Now all those companies have been amalgamated into four huge corporations, and standardisation is producing, to my vision, a dull uniformity. Sir Josiah Stamp recently visualised the time when the great railway over which he presides may boast only 20 types of locomotive. Several years ago it took over, from the various companies which it absorbed, nearly 400 types! As a businessman, Sir Josiah spoke with reasonable pride. But I should not wonder if there be something of the boy left even in himself, and if that part of him lament the decline in picturesqueness which modern industry demands. I deplore it, at any rate; and I grieve to think that, by the time you are seven or eight, our trains may be almost as indistinguishable from one another as the efficient and comfortable—but oh, how prosy!—trains of Germany.

I foresee only one advantage—and that a questionable one —in the new conditions. If you should ever build up piece-meal a model railway, as I did in my early teens, you will be less distracted by a conflict of loyalties. With 16 main companies in the field, I could sustain undisputable enthusiasm for none of them. As our annual family holiday, or the occasional business trips upon which I accompanied my father, took me to different parts of the country, I favoured successively each new railway upon which I travelled, until my miniature line might have carried replicas of more companies' rolling-stock, had such replicas then been obtainable, than were seen in actuality upon the old Highland system itself. When you come to buying rolling-stock for your model railway, selection from originals will offer less difficulty—if also, I cannot help feeling, less fun.

And yet, since you will lack my memories, railways may seem to you as romantic as they once seemed to me. You will be vaguely interested when I talk of the white-and-chocolate coaches of the old North Western, the blue locomotives of the late Caledonian, or the graceful Atlantics which used to haul the *Flying Scotsman* between London and York, and for which I find the modern 'hush-hush' engines a poor æsthetic substitute. You will, I say, be vaguely interested, as I was in boyhood when my own father told how, when first travelling to London in *his* boyhood, he rode by stage-coach from his Monmouthshire village to Chepstow, where he joined the old broad-gauge train that stopped at every station and made the compulsory 20 minutes' halt at Swindon. I recall, again, his description of the old Bishopsgate terminus of the Great Eastern in London, and of how, when he arrived there on a night of pea-soup fog, the porters walked about the platforms carrying torches. Such stories have historical vitality for me now. But, when I was young, they lacked what the young demand—the stab of actuality. Similarly, my recollections will stir you but dimly when, in a few years' time, we potter together about some railway station; and you will think me a little mad when you hear me passionately declaiming, in misquotation of Francis Thompson,

O my King's Cross and my Euston long ago!

THE HOLE

If real railways inspire affection for model ones, models in turn prompt fresh love of the prototypes. And in Hertfordshire, as previously in Essex, we were fortunate in being but a few minutes' walk from a scene of considerable railway interest, with (this time) a pleasing natural setting.

Near our house, which stood a mile from the town, our road crossed a picturesque cutting in which lay the four-fold track of the LMS main line from St Pancras. Just north of the bridge was a double crossover, connecting the fast lines with the slow; and, some hundreds of yards further off, the cutting veered gracefully out of view. As we gazed over the parapet of our rural bridge, we could hear the up trains long before they swept round the curve into sight, though from the movements of the arms on the tall bracket-signal, if not earlier from our calculation of the speed of the still-invisible oncomer, we could tell whether a train was to continue on the fast road or was to pass, as many locals or semi-expresses did at this point, to the slow.

Then, just under us, a single-line branch turned off the

main down fast track, and disappeared round the bend of its own pretty cutting. Thrice daily, in each direction, this branch was used by a train consisting of a tank engine and a passenger coach, which ran between our own station and one, some miles across country, on the trunk of the old LNWR. How the youngsters loved that little train, whose solitary carriage never seemed to carry more than the same few schoolchildren and working men, one of whom always sat comfortably reading his newspaper, not only in the guard's compartment but in the guard's seat. How the engine squeaked as it turned into or out of the branch; and what fun it was to see the signalman descend the steps of his cabin to give or receive the token without the locomotive's quite stopping.

When coming off the branch the train had, of course, to traverse the down fast main line for some yards before taking its own special crossover to the up fast, on reaching which it puffed energetically toward our local station, as if proud of being, if only for a few minutes, on the express road. David was sometimes apprehensive lest, ere this operation was completed, the little train should be hit by a down flier. His knowledge of the actual safeguards exceeded, as yet, his faith in their dependability. And, indeed, the short interval that might elapse between the clearing of the branch train and the passage of an express in full career, over the same strip of metals but in the opposite direction, was enough to make any adult hold his breath.

If we crossed the bridge and then, turning northward, followed the main line, we soon came to a spot where some fields fell steeply to form a snug little hollow sheer beside the railway. We affectionately called this The Hole. There, sitting on the fence, while we listened to the skylark and watched the rabbits frisking in the spinney on the opposite bank of the cutting, we had a magnificent view of the expresses as they raced into or out of sight round yet another beautiful curve. Not only so: at this very spot the seemingly interminable coal-trains of this line were often halted by signal. We had the excitement of watching, to the accompaniment of clanging buffers, their laborious stopping and starting, and enjoyed many a conversation with their engine-crews. Our daughter was specially proud when honoured by the driver or fireman of one of the huge Garrett-articulated locomotives, though she was less successful in pronouncing the name than in distinguishing, even at a distance, the type. So regular was our appearance at The Hole that even some express engine-men waved to us with the unmistakable gesture of recognition. On one occasion, when his fireman was busy feeding the furnace, a driver, spotting us, gave his mate such a prod that the shovel fell from his hand, and the bewildered fellow looked up, as if in expectation of impending calamity; till, having been made to understand the cause of his buffeting, he too was just in time to hail us as his fiery steed, bound for Manchester, vanished round the corner.

Despite The Hole, the children's allegiance to the Great Western, which they had still to see 'in the flesh', remained unshaken. So did mine. But I should have been less than human if sometimes, during solitary half-hours, I had not fallen into a mood of wistful reminiscence. As we grow older, we cannot but feel a certain tenderness for the things that were familiar in childhood, even if at the time they did not completely satisfy us; and here, on the route from St Pancras to Leicester, I was back on my native line—the good, solid, comfortable, unromantic Midland. Nor had it changed quite so much as had many other railways: the LMS had at least retained the crimson livery. But, fine as was the rolling-stock, I sighed for the clerestory coaches of former days. Were more handsome vehicles ever built? As for the engines, these were now larger and more powerful, and some of them were even named. Yet such is human perversity that, sitting in The Hole, I found myself thinking how delightful it would be to see one of the old single-drivers come striding along.

Is it just sentimental regret for the past, or is it a maturer æsthetic judgement, that makes me endorse Mr E. W.

Twining's opinion that 'for pure beauty of outline, finish and painting'—to which might be added cleanliness and polish—'the locomotives of the latter part of the nineteenth century were unsurpassed'; that 'designers such as Samuel W. Johnson on the Midland, Benjamin Conner and Drummond on the Caledonian, William Dean on the Great Western, Patrick Stirling on the Great Northern, William Stroudley on the London, Brighton & South Coast, and many others, were supreme artists in metal-work'?

I do not wonder that many model-lovers, inspired by the charm of those old engines, run a 'period' railway. Not only is there the artistic and historical appeal, but to live imaginatively in the past is to be immune from the uncertainties of the ever-changing present. That they can keep the past alive is another virtue of models, and I warmly support a recent plea for the establishment of a model-railway museum, in which every bygone type of locomotive, rolling-stock and other railway equipment could be represented and preserved in miniature.

Sometimes I am disposed to regret that I did not make my own line a 'period' one. But the possibilities of model railways are so many that, having launched upon a certain course, it is wise to pursue it without indulging laments that one did not do something else. And when I look at my models of the locomotives *King George V*, *Pendennis Castle* and *Llanvair Grange*, I appreciate that there is, after all, much to be said for the present. How long, in this era of upheaval, the 'present' will remain the present is, of course, another matter. The early future threatens or promises—the reader, according to his political or other views, may choose which of the two verbs he prefers—to bring more sweeping changes to our railways. If these changes should materialise—bringing, from the æsthetic and sentimental points of view, a dull uniformity, whatever might be the possible merits on other counts—then indeed our model railway would become a 'period' one.

BETWEEN COURSES

In May 1937, a decision having been taken to settle in the
Westcountry, the family took a holiday by road, prospecting
for a home. It happened that our chauffeur-friend shared our
own passion for railways. The only bone of contention was
that he professed a sneaking admiration for the Southern
system, whereas we were all Great Western fans. Excitement
was intensified because, while this was my own return to
Great Western territory after abnormally long absence, it was
David's first actual introduction. Whenever our road crossed
or ran alongside its tracks—we affected to pass the Southern
lines with a lofty scorn—we waited to see a train and to catch
the name of its engine; and, by a curiously happy coincidence,
the first named locomotive we 'bagged' was none other than
the famous *Caerphilly Castle*, prototype of the miniature at

home. Against the children's importunity our helmsman was adamant when risks would be involved. But he gave us some thrilling races after trains when a safe road made it possible; and, to show what he could do in a good cause, he several times overtook expresses travelling at high speed. Nor will David forget the circumstances in which he first saw his fabled train of trains.

Other considerations apart, I have found that nowhere in a large city may you eat more comfortably—or more quietly— than in the station restaurant; nor, by going there, do you waste half an hour in looking for a car-park. Thus, one day, we sat over our roast chicken in the secluded dining-room at St David's, Exeter, when, glancing at the clock, I realised that the down *Cornish Riviera Limited* was almost due to begin its ten minutes' stop at the adjoining platform. Yet if to miss seeing it would be a crime, to go without our sweets and cheese would be a misfortune. Summoning the waitress, I explained the situation and offered to leave a deposit, which she graciously refused. So, between the courses, we filed out of the room. Half a minute before time, the *Limited*, hauled by *King Henry VII*, drew into the station, nonchalantly as if having run non-stop from Paddington in less than three hours were the merest bagatelle. After we had strolled from end to end of the train, immaculate in its chocolate-and-cream livery, and after Ruth's health had been drunk by a gallant gentleman in the diner, whose eyes she had caught from her vantage-point in her mother's arms, we had time for a word with the driver, whose opinion of the feminine sex manifestly rose when my wife admired the 'beauty' of his steed. Then, *King Henry VII* having started on the next (and most difficult) stage of the journey to Plymouth, we returned to the dining-room to find the gooseberry tart and cream already on our plates and a still sweeter smile on the face of the motherly waitress.

TEMPLE MEADS

I have been reading Canon Roger Lloyd's book *The Fascination of Railways*. Its appeal is to those who, like himself and like me, know and care nothing about 'such mysteries as super-heating, saturated steam, valves, and so forth'. Incidentally, as showing the popularity of his theme, Canon Lloyd says: 'If I write three articles, one about religion, one about some literary or historical subject, and one about the romance of railways or some trivial detail of their working, I shall receive four or five times as many letters about the railway article as about the other two together'. This exactly describes my own experience.

For Canon Lloyd, as for countless others, the spell of railways is easier to feel than to define. It is, I suppose, the many-sidedness of railways that breeds so many devotees. People love them for different reasons. One common link is affection for the steam locomotive, whether there is technical knowledge or a complete ignorance of mechanical first principles. The steam locomotive is the one really civilised machine devised by man. It is safe and dependable in all weathers; it is powerful enough to be slightly awe-inspiring, yet tame and gentle enough to be friendly; it has living and visible breath; it screams, sings, pants, or purrs according to its task at the moment; it is companionable. It deserves the romantic names often bestowed upon it. Who would dream of giving such names—equally fitting when they suggest masculine force or feminine grace—to electric-train motor-units or to the diesel locomotives that are now appearing on some main lines? Still, the love of railways will survive the eventual passing of steam, and it extends to the modern young, who have been brought up with other forms of transport, no less than to us elders for whom in childhood the railway held a monopoly, and was therefore associated with our early exploration of the world.

One of Canon Lloyd's best chapters is on 'station sauntering', and his early recollections emotionally confirm mine, though Whitchurch in Shropshire was the station toward which he tugged a reluctant mother or nurse, while the Midland station at Leicester was my paradise. At Cambridge we joined hands, if across half a generation. On that crazy station, with its single through platform of fantastic length, he, as an undergraduate, spent enchanted afternoons, watching the same traffic movements I witnessed, some years earlier, as a boy at The Leys School, shamelessly breaking bounds. But in my time the 'Hamilton' locomotives, resplendent in blue livery, still hauled the Great Eastern expresses, while into the bay platforms came trains of the Great Northern, London & North Western and Midland companies, offering a feast of varied form and hue.

Edinburgh (Waverley); Glasgow (St Enoch); Carlisle (Citadel); Hull (Paragon); Plymouth (Friary); Exeter (St David's);

Dover (Friary); London (St Pancras). What music there is in our railway station names, and how pleasantly they link present with past! On all of these stations except Paragon, as on dozens more, I have sauntered at one time or another; but specially dear to me, both for its name and for personal associations, is Bristol (Temple Meads).

Among my most cherished memories is that of the day when, a small boy, I first stepped out of our Midland train— it was the old station then, dirty and cramped and (rather perplexingly) having platforms on both sides of one running track—and beheld the GW coaches. Was it their colour as such that thrilled me, or did my exiled Western blood take fire from the knowledge that I was changing to the GWR? Anyhow, the recollection has persisted, and never in later years did I pass through Temple Meads without feeling that westward the land was bright. Temple Meads might not itself be the goal of my dreams; but it was the jumping-off point, and anticipation was quickened by the sensation of changing from one very distinctive railway to another. I am sorry for the children of today, enjoying no such vivid contrast.

I was at Temple Meads again recently. I travelled up in a compartment near the engine, and not for some years had I sat behind a locomotive that seemed to be so thoroughly enjoying a job of which it was fully master. Its even, happy breathing while running at speed was a joy to hear; the ease with which it started its 14 coaches, accelerated after a PW slack or climbed the bank to Whiteball Tunnel, were equally pleasing. At Bristol I had a word with Driver Pattenden, who, at his home town of Newton Abbot, had taken over the train on its arrival from Plymouth, and was working it to Shrewsbury *en route* for Manchester. His rosy face broke into a quiet smile when I congratulated him on a good run, but the smile became a beam when I added that his engine seemed to be in fine fettle. With a roguish chuckle, he told me I was right. Only a few days previously *Llantillo Castle* had drawn Royalty, and had been suitably overhauled for the occasion.

TEIGNMOUTH SEA WALL CONTRAST. Top: *The frontispiece of Charles H. Grinling's 'The Ways of Our Railways' (1910), one of the first books bought by the author (Part One). The caption stated that the 'Cornish Riviera Express' 'runs from Paddington to Plymouth without a stop—246 miles in 265 minutes'. Bottom: The 1963 'Cornish Riviera' which takes 255 minutes to reach Plymouth by the shorter route of 226 miles. It makes two intermediate stops*

MID-DEVON BRANCHES. *Moretonhampstead line's last day, 28 February 1959, and at Dunsford Halt, Teign Valley branch, March 1958*

Having done the business that took me to Bristol, I decided, before returning home, to spend an hour or two on the station. If all big stations are fascinating, not all are as spacious, comfortable, and 'friendly' as Temple Meads, with its sound, simple architecture and curving platforms. For a time I was absorbed in watching the trains, observing the layout of the tracks, and noting details of railway working; and I found all this no less engrossing because I had done it, at this same spot, many times before. Novelty may be the spice of life; familiarity —for myself—is its meat.

Though there come comparatively long lulls, when a Sabbath-like calm settles upon the scene, there is plenty doing at Temple Meads; and, like every large station, it has its own atmosphere and its own peculiar traffic movements. In one respect there is less activity than at some important—or even smaller—stations. While Bristol is a great centre for the interchange of passengers, there is little breaking up and joining together of trains. Locals in abundance begin and end their journeys here, as also, in their own terminal bay, do the LMR services to and from the Midlands and the North. But most of the Western expresses pass through the main platforms without adding or shedding more than a horse-box or other odd vehicle, brought in or fetched away by a little pannier-tank engine that appears, as if by magic, at the psychological moment. Magic? No! Yet what foresight and finely dovetailed organisation are needed to make possible the smooth carrying out even of so small an operation!

In few stations of comparable size is one less conscious of the dominance of London. The faster trains from Paddington to the West of England have for some 40 years used the short cut *via* Westbury, while those from Paddington to South Wales the route *via* Badminton. For London—as also for South Wales—Temple Meads has to provide special services, though some of the London trains begin or end their runs at Weston-super-Mare. At regular intervals a train for Paddington draws in to platform nine; but so much more characteristic

75

are the long-distance cross-country expresses linking South West with North—expresses formerly combining GW and LMS stock—that the Capital, little more than a hundred miles away, seems relatively unimportant. Bristol reigns as a metropolis herself.

Sitting on platform nine, I found myself retaking many happy journeys over half a century. Then, by one of those sudden flights in which imagination rejoices, I was transported to pre-railway times. I thought of the Saxon settlement at 'Brigstow'; of the Danes, who began the wool trade with Ireland and made Bristol a market for English slaves; of the growing commerce of the chartered city with France, Spain and the Levant; of, among so much else, the Revival of the Wesleys that forms as bright a page of Bristolian history as its traffic in African slaves for the West Indies, in exchange for sugar and rum, makes a dark one.

On or near the site of Temple Meads station lay, presumably, the meadows of the once-independent rural district of Temple, where the Templars held the manor in feudal times. As a goods train drew into one of the middle roads between the main up platforms, and as its long string of wagons (their varied freight attesting the complexity of modern civilisation) came to a clanging stop before an 'on' signal, it seemed a far cry back to the days of the Poor Knights of Christ, who, forsaking worldly chivalry, vowed themselves, with chastity, obedience and poverty, 'to fight with a pure mind for the supreme and true King'. Fancy likes to see those knights in their original simplicity, when, not yet having a regular habit, they wore whatever garments charity might bring them. Yet I suspect that when the Templars settled outside Bristol, their Order had already forgotten its early ideals, and was in process of becoming one of the wealthiest, most powerful and most militant in Europe. However that may be, Temple Meads suggests a religious foundation, and there, though the meadows have long since gone, I still find something of a shrine.

I can again confirm Canon Lloyd when he says not only that talk with railwaymen remarkably often becomes 'a discussion on organists and choirs and places where they sing', but that there seems some 'general kinship between the religious view of life and the railway scene'. For myself, I never remain long at any great railway centre before interest in the railway itself turns to reverie, and reverie, a little later, to positive meditation. Nor is this strange. With the vision of God must go a vision of humanity; and where better can we catch this latter vision than in a railway station, with multifarious human types and needs passing vividly (sometimes poignantly) before our eyes? The nearby spire of St Mary Redcliffe may point the Way and the End; but Temple Meads reminds us that eternity is fashioned through the traffic of time.

The clock, however, warned me that my return train was almost due. As I passed along the subway, with its colourful display windows, to platform five, I wondered what engine would take me home. It would not be *Llantillo Castle*, which I pictured Driver Pattenden affectionately stabling for the night in Shrewsbury shed.

(*Pictures page 55*)

PADDINGTON TO SEAGOOD

In 1939 we settled in a small coastal town in South Devon. It was an added satisfaction that we should now be living on the real Great Western Railway and at a place where the famous sea wall is a constant reminder of the genius of its begetter, Isambard Kingdom Brunel, the poet-engineer.

Profiting by our experience in Hertfordshire, we asked, on arrival here, to be shown no post-1914 property. We were fortunate in finding a suitable house, with (for the railway) a large billiards-room, which, of impressively solid structure, had been added to the original edifice. Model-railway engineers are notoriously avid of 'acreage'; but I could hardly myself have planned a more desirable apartment. Measuring some 27 ft by 19½, it is spacious, perfectly rectangular and sunny, and, thanks to the slope of the land, it has an uncommon feature. One door opens into the garden, while another, leading into the house, is reached by a flight of stairs, from the top of which a bird's-eye view of the whole layout is obtainable.

Our first layout on the new site was completed in the early summer of 1939. It remained substantially unchanged until 1945. So far as working a large and varied amount of traffic was concerned—and that, after all, is the vital test—it proved, on the whole, very satisfactory. While the double track made it possible for trains to be run simultaneously in opposite directions, trains of different kinds, travelling in the same direction, could overtake one another; while every common type of shunting operation, passenger or goods, could be effected without an insoluble muddle—or, as a rule, any muddle at all—arising.

Nevertheless, soon after the layout was finished, I realised that I had not taken full advantage of my space. Apart from some short but lamentable sections of 3-ft curve on the main line, most of the goods reception roads and shunting spurs limited trains to ten wagons. This did not matter in principle, since the pleasure of model railroading consists, I would repeat, not in slavish imitation of the real thing, but in essential fidelity to actual working conditions. No model line in O-gauge can cope, like a real railway, with trains of 15 coaches or 100 wagons; and, if it could, the assembling of them would be very tedious! It is from carrying out *representative* railway operations that the interest springs, and this may be done quite satisfactorily on a diminutive scale. Were I necessarily restricted to running short trains, my zest for the hobby would not radically be lessened.

When, on the other hand, one's space permits of longer trains, and when one's locomotives will haul them, one naturally asks why one should continue to accept needless limitations; and, had not war come, I should not have waited long before undertaking revisions. Yet there is something to be said for not being precipitate. One learns much by working a reasonably sound, if far from perfect, system over a lengthy period; and, for myself, I prefer an occasional major upheaval to a constant series of minor ones.

Had it been possible to start again from scratch, with the

experience I had now gained, I might, as on a still-earlier occasion, have considered a totally different layout. But the development of a model railway, like that of a real one, is controlled in large measure by its original scheme, and, on the whole, I did not seriously regret being committed to a comprehensive system. The design and working of such a system, as an organic whole, has always fascinated me. Anyhow, my large amount of equipment and rolling-stock compelled me to reap as I had sowed, and the proposed changes were intended merely to give better expression to the same fundamental idea. Moreover, the existing benches, as I have said, were built so ultra-strongly against the walls of the room that I deemed it prudent to cause the least possible disturbance.

Though I had no thought of getting to work until peace returned, I began drawing plans as early as 1940, and, while supplies were still available, ordered the small amount of additional track, including several special formations, that would obviously be needed. The re-planning on paper, enjoyed for its own sake no less than as a promise of the fruit it might ultimately bear, gave me many scattered hours of pleasure and of relief from the strain and gloom of the war years. Much of it was done while we took shelter at night in our cellar during air raids, of which, for its size, our little town had more than its share. In the summer of 1942, indeed, the daylight 'tip and runs' became so bad that we migrated for a time to North Devon. It was a sad day when we packed the locomotives away in the most suitable cupboard in the house. The layout as a whole, with the rest of the rolling-stock, was left *in situ*. Happily the house was undamaged. The only thing that went wrong during our 20 months' absence was that a number of wagon wheels had become loose on their axles. This may conceivably have been due to heat or cold— or both. Normally, with a gas radiator in winter and green blinds as a defence against the very strong sunlight in summer, we manage to keep the railway room at a fairly even temperature.

While in exile I wrote for the *Model Railway News* an article in which I set out what I then thought were my final plans for the post-war layout. Actually, however, when we returned home and the wheels of our railway began to revolve again, I made considerable changes in the design, after further study of the problem on the spot. The scheme at length adopted and carried into effect during the early months of 1945, after the base-board had received a darker coat of paint —we had previously made the mistake of having it too light— is shown in the accompanying diagram.

The first major improvement is that the minimum curve on main lines, with one partial exception to be mentioned later, is of 4-ft radius. Desirable in themselves as yet more generous curves may be, they would in any case have been hard to reconcile with my idea of a comprehensive system, even if the trestles could entirely have been rearranged. Since this latter operation would have involved undue expense and upheaval, I so contrived matters that, while three benches were broadened with extra planks—still leaving abundant operating space—only a short section of baseboard that previously carried the line from the oval to the small terminus, 'Seagood', had to undergo 'surgical' treatment. This section has been moved to the other end of the room, where it now carries the track from the oval into 'Paddington' which, though facing in the opposite direction, occupies the site formerly held by 'Seagood'.

The interchange of locations between the two termini was unavoidable if 4-ft curves on the oval and along the approaches to 'Paddington' were to be attained without drastic disturbance of the trestles. Yet from every other point of view— including that of providing the maximum possible end-to-end run—this interchange has been to the good. The peninsular bench in the middle of the room might seem to be the obvious position for the main terminus; but in fact, slow as I had been in awakening to it, the aggregate space offered by the 'peninsula' is less ample than that provided by the old 'Sea-

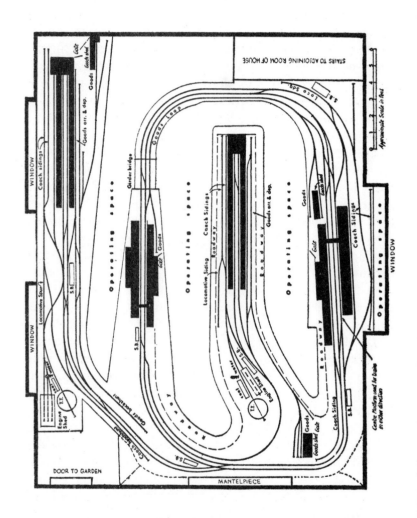

82

good' bench (with its greater length) as now widened by a gradual slope outwards, along part of its course.

The new 'Paddington' layout is a vast improvement on the old. There are longer sidings and better facilities for locomotives, with direct access, by means of a special track formation, from the passenger station to the turntable, over which engines no longer have to travel (as formerly) in order to reach the three-road shed. The 'passenger' shunting spur, between which and the coach sidings there is direct connection, leaving the main line free, is of generous length, though from the main line there is alternative entry to the coach sidings by means of a track that also offers locomotives another exit from their own depot. The goods reception and departure line, which has a useful back-shunt, is now thoroughly adequate, and there is easy exit for engines of arriving freighters. The goods shunting at 'Paddington' is now done by the 'Dean', permanently stationed there; while the pannier 'tank' undertakes the 'passenger' shunting.

A notable feature at this revised terminus is the new signal-box, which, from a narrow base, overlaps the track on either side. This cabin (suitably adapted) was made by Messrs Bassett-Lowke from an official drawing of Birmingham (Snow Hill) North Box, kindly supplied by the GWR. The line from the oval to 'Paddington'—the trains look very graceful as they wind around the curves—was deliberately made circuitous for two reasons. Firstly, the terminal section is made to appear more remote: the illusion of distance is given. Secondly, I wanted to ensure that, at the double junction, the straight route should be that taken by trains traversing the oval. . . .

Leaving 'Paddington' and entering the oval, we reach the 'junction' station. On a widened bench, this occupies its old site; but considerable alterations have been made. The central of the three tracks between the platforms remains a 'through' road for down trains, while, as before, the down platform is served by a loop. The inner side of the island platform, however, can now be used for traffic in both directions, like the middle platform at Carlisle. This arrangement has added much to working possibilities and interest, and the layout is so devised as not to interfere with the free passage of non-stopping expresses. Thus, while a stopping down train is crossing to the inner side of the island platform, an up express can proceed at full speed along its own fast track on the outer side. Though there is plenty of room for trains to draw up when necessary, the old six-feet-long island platform is still in use, but will now be extended at the first opportunity. The long 'passenger' shunting loop, which can also serve on occasion as a temporary siding, should not be overlooked. The large signal-box originally built for 'Paddington' guards the eastern approaches to this station, while a smaller box, formerly at 'Seagood', is placed at the western end. The goods-yard now possesses a depot, which it previously lacked.

The working of goods traffic at the 'junction' station has been greatly facilitated. The entry of down freight trains to their own shunting spur remains as before: it could not be more direct. But up trains now have an easier route, for a new three-road crossover, intersecting the down 'main', has been installed from the middle passenger platform direct to the shunting spur. This spur now holds much longer trains. It is, indeed, a loop, extending beyond the girder bridge. It thus provides direct exit for down goods trains leaving the 'junction' station. This same spur or loop also serves as goods siding at the smaller intermediate, or 'country', station, where, though freight trains are legitimately shunted from the main line, a back-shunt is needed for the actual vehicles to be dropped or picked up.

This sharing by two stations of the same shunting track may possibly have its counterpart in actual practice, though in that case the track would be divided by signals into sections. The length and the curves of this spur or loop on our own model line virtually conceal, except from over-prying eyes, the fact of its *being* continuous. Anyway, this arrangement, so usefully saving of space, is, I feel, not so much a fundamental breach of realism as a justifiable taking of poetic licence.

It was necessary to widen the bench carrying the 'country' station in order that the sweep round into the smaller terminus might be adequate. The 'country' station therefore now stands at a slightly different angle and has a wider roadway approach. Otherwise, save for the different provision for goods shunting above described, it remains as before. From the western end of this station a single track takes off for 'Seagood'. Trains, however, are still split up or joined, when required, at the 'junction' station.

The track leading to 'Seagood' (owing, again, to the original disposition of the trestles) inevitably has some sections of 3-ft curve, sandwiched between 4-ft ones. As we still regard 'Seagood' as being a smallish coastal terminus, I have not elaborated arrangements here. 'Passenger' shunting—permissable at a station of this type—is carried out from the main line. A crossover within the station enables the main-line locomotive to run round its train and to do the shunting at need. It is, however, normally performed by a 'resident' pilot, which often, though not of necessity, is used for goods shunting. Both platforms at 'Seagood' are now of full length; there are two ample coach sidings; while there is full accommodation for the moderate amount of freight traffic reaching this outlying dead-end. . . .

At the moment of writing, owing to the continued lack of supplies, we are still having to make shift with existing signals, which do not in every case strictly 'match' the changed locations; and there are other little 'creases' to be ironed out as soon as conditions permit. Substantially, however, the new layout is complete within the limits aimed at. Having worked it for nine months, we are satisfied that the 'foundations' of the railway have at last been well and truly laid. No further major alterations are now anticipated. But on a model system, as on a real one, there always remains scope for improved buildings, locomotives, rolling-stock and the like.

Some day, we promise ourselves, we will ballast the track. A little temporary and experimental ballasting of one section was, indeed, carried out some years ago. There is no denying the improved appearance which ballasting produces. Nevertheless, the ballasting of a complicated system is a big (and sticky!) job, and so far we have shirked it. Nor have we yet aspired to the mechanical operation of points and signals, which would involve expense and effort disproportionate to the satisfaction it would afford ourselves, whose main interest does not lie in that department.

As for scenery: we are convinced that this, unless supremely well done, reduces rather than increases realism. Not only does the introduction of scenery call for great constructive skill: it demands faultless artistic judgement. This in turn raises the whole question of balance: the relation between the scenery and the railway. An extensive model system in O-gauge would need vast space if the scenery were not to be out of proportion and perspective. Alternatively, in a restricted space, the railway itself must be considerably reduced in size—or much of it hidden from view, with the resulting working difficulties and the diminution of purely railway appeal—if the scenery is really to harmonise with the layout.

Much may be done by a discreet array of actual railway buildings or other features to suggest the kind of rural or urban district through which a particular section of line is conceived to be traversing; and of such buildings and features, including retaining walls, which we hope in due course to add here and there to our own system, there is no lack of choice. But, unless accommodation be superabundant, or unless one is willing to limit the range of one's trackage, certain railway features themselves, such as tunnels, may best be omitted when these inherently demand a modelled natural setting, and an extensive one at that. On this matter, it seems to me, no less an authority than Mr William C. Boulton* has spoken the final word of wisdom, though I may be biased

* See *The Model Railway News*, June, 1942

because, while we are personally unacquainted, he chose some photographs of the Paddington to Seagood Railway to prove his point!

For myself, in any case, I want a part-time hobby, not a full-time occupation: a model railway, not a model universe. Equally it must be borne in mind that the younger elements on the 'board' may, in coming years, have an increasing influence on 'policy'.

All future schemes, however, are in the lap of the gods. Only one thing is certain: the gods themselves cannot recall the gifts already bestowed. Meanwhile, the existing railway continues to yield good 'dividends'. The popular slogan of the hobby is 'Always complete, but never finished'. Happily, the emphasis can be reversed. An adequate model line, if not finished, is nevertheless complete; and while the mind receives freedom and stimulus from contemplating the mere possibility of further advance—while one does not move in a closed circle, as in some pastimes—a modest measure of success, once achieved, brings delights that do not easily pall.

(Pictures pages 163 and 164)

NOSTALGIA

(For Railway Lovers Only)

You loved them too: those locos motley gay
That once seemed permanent as their own way?—
The Midland 'lake', the Caledonian blue;
The Brighton 'Stroudleys' in their umber hue;
North-Western 'Jumbos', shimmeringly black,
That sped, shrill-whistled, on their 'Premier' track;
And all a forest's tints of green—G.C.,
G.N., G.W., L.T.S., H.B.,
South Western, Highland, 'Chatham': many more
Both on our own and on the Emerald shore?
Did you, beneath a sooty Oldham sky,
Think dour the 'Aspinalls' of L. and Y.,

NOSTALGIA

Or, in the gloom of the Five Towns, admire
The cheerful, sturdy, red North Staffordshire?
Do you remember how the Suffolk sun
Gleamed on a blue Great Eastern 'Hamilton'?
In Wessex did you keep slow company
With the 'tanks' (royal) of the S. and D.,
That waited, as it seemed, for crack of doom
(While they performed strange rites) at Templecombe?
Across the Fens and Broadland did you reach,
And come—in course of time—to Cromer (Beach)
Behind a khaki M. and G.N.J.,
And was the 'pea soup' to your liking—say!—
Of the N.B. that took us over Forth
On our first wizard journey Further North?

The Johnson 'singles', Drummond 4—4—0's!
Were ever engines lovelier than those?
What treasured names they bore—*Sir Francis Drake,*
Swallow, Lysander, Lady of the Lake,
Courier, Gladstone, Glowworm, Lorna Doone,
Titan, Apollo, Jeannie Deans, Typhoon!
And in their wake what rainbow splendour ran:
The bronze-green coaches of the Cambrian;
G.N.S. red and white; North Eastern 'plum';
'Salmon' that struck one young observer dumb
At grim old Waterloo; the varnished teak
That, North or South, was never far to seek,
But had for apogee East Coast Joint Stock
That left King's Cross each morning, ten o'clock—
Though many held this did not equal quite
The West Coast purple-brown and 'spilt milk' white.

Those Furness trains—red, white, and blue—at Grange?
That 'orange' touch at Liverpool (Exchange);
At Central the dark oak of Cheshire Lines?
Or—what the memory most of all enshrines:

NOSTALGIA

The crown and consummation of our dreams—
Those great 'joint' hubs where many colour schemes
Converged to hold us under such a spell:
York, Cambridge, Perth, or Carlisle (Citadel)? . . .
The high 'birdcages' of L.C. and D.?
Those dismal Broad Street arks one used to see
Above one ere, in hardly prouder state,
One trundled up the bank at Bishopsgate? . . .
Those little Emett lines which 'also ran',
Saucily mocking at the march of man—
Festiniog, Southwold, Wantage, Isle of Wight,
Lynton and Barnstaple, East Suffolk Light? . . .
Yes, I remember! But I will not flog
My muse to furnish the whole catalogue.

Variety itself could more enthrall
Because we held—'belovèd over all'—
Each our own choice. Although my youth was bred
Amid the comfortable Midland red,
And though for long, wherever I might roam,
M.R. to me spelled certitude and home,
Yet all my exiled Western blood took fire
When—a small boy in snowy-starched attire—
I first changed trains at Bristol (Temple Meads).
Awhile my tastes were fickle; but the seeds
Sown there have proved the stubbornest by far:
Upon my heart is graved G.W.R.
And when I came to live near Brunel's wall,
Between the red cliffs and the rise and fall
Of Devon waves, I thought long years to see,
In ever more familiar livery,
The 'Dutchman' or the 'Limited' swing by,
Washed by the Channel spray.

                    Hope born to die!

DAINTON BANK. Top: *'Hall' class No. 4984 storms up from Stoney-combe on Sunday 16 April 1961.* Bottom: *'King Edward VIII' between Stoneycombe and Dainton, 17 February 1957*

A CORNISH BYWAY. Top: *Beattie tank 2—4—0 at the water tower on the Wenford Bridge freight branch in November 1953.* Bottom: *At the china clay works later on the same trip*

PART 2 by DAVID St JOHN THOMAS

FRIEND OR FOE?

How did I become a railway enthusiast? I have been asked the question hundreds of times, and have never yet been able to answer satisfactorily. I just grew up as one; I take it as much for granted as I do the family and the morning newspaper. The interest in railways forms such an integral part of life that when asked about hobbies I sometimes forget to mention it, listing only lesser pastimes.

The start of the interest was natural enough. In my child-hood we had the Paddington to Seagood model railway; we frequently travelled by train; our visitors included people of all types who talked about railways past and present. In early 'teens, railways dominated my reading matter, *Railway Wonders of the World* being my invariable companion during wartime nocturnal sessions in the cellar. A dampish, claustro-phobic smell still automatically reminds me of that splendid two-volume tome.

After the war I began the discovery of Britain by train, and a grand education this was. In four years I was given not merely some first-hand knowledge of much of the railway sys-tem of England and Wales (Scotland was a joy to come later), but the chance to explore countless towns, villages, cathedrals, market places, promenades and bookshops. The posters still say 'See Britain by Train', but full exploration as distinct from through journeys has often become impossible; and generally, even where stopping services survive, they are no longer the pivot of local life. A mere 15 years ago a journey in the guard's van on one of a branch's busier passenger trains could give a good insight into a valley's economy and sociology.

Spare time offered the model railway and weekend visits to signalboxes. At 15 I knew signalmen in several boxes who allowed me to do their job, under supervision, except answer the telephone. It was joy unsurpassed to stand over the levers duster in hand as the *Cornish Riviera Express* thundered through Dawlish, or—yet more satisfying—to be allowed to celebrate the whole ritual of crossing trains at a station on a single-track branch.

Aged 16, I had a thrill of another kind. My first article, sub-mitted secretly, was accepted by the Press, almost as much to my embarrassment as surprise. 'Brunel Was Too Optimistic Says David St J. Thomas', declared the heading. As my English master pointed out acidly when shown the four-column spread, I had not yet taken school certificate. While in the sixth form I began writing regular topical comment on the railway situation. The question then arose whether I should join the railway service. A job on the GWR was kept open for one agonising week. Instead, I began as junior reporter at *The Western Morning News* Plymouth head office. Here I was lucky. The West Country public's interest in railways was well understood, and stories about unusual excursions, timetable changes, centenaries and motive-power problems were assured of a corner of honour. A keen demand was found for 'gossip pars', on such matters as the staff's nicknames for different trains, trains which failed to stop at scheduled stations, and Cossington station on the old Somerset & Dorset which should not have been closed because an unrepealed Act of Parliament dictated that it should be maintained 'for ever hereafter'.

The railway officials who might have taken scant notice of a junior on their staff allowed the Press free tickets to write up special events and granted wishes such as to see Plymouth's railways at night, to ride on the Travelling Post Office, and to explore branches used only by mineral traffic. Finding me conversant with affairs behind the scenes, engine drivers and stationmasters were the more ready to talk. In the days before enthusiasts were on the prowl *en masse* I collected a vast quantity of lore and legend.

The railway system was a unique institution, rendering the West Country great services—such as expanding tourism after the war—for which the usual return was criticisms about trivialities. Loyalty among the staff was exceptional; the sheer technical achievements were often magnificent. West Country railways were a matter of immense pride, and their worth deserved public notice. Yet the wheels were clogging. Having regained pre-war standards, the railways stood still while the nation's economy forged ahead and road traffic thickened. Staff morale sank as initiative was suppressed, and traffic was allowed to drift away without any fight to retain it —or to cut costs once it had gone.

One day I would write a report extolling some complex

piece of organisation and forget the debit side; the next it seemed but common sense to call attention to some appalling waste of resources in the hope that ridicule might elicit remedy.

Friend or foe? How could I most constructively use background knowledge? People with a vested interest in denigrating railways—and there are many such—must have chuckled at some reports. Yet the airing of specific grievances did directly lead to action—even, sometimes, after Paddington or Waterloo had denied the allegations or the possibility of rectification.

Perhaps it was—and is—something like being in love with a wayward woman. Admiration for much of what the railways accomplish as well as sheer love of their curves and stations and locomotives burns undiminished. But to many of us the folly of their ways is an incessant harassment. A friend circulates duplicated timetable details among his neighbours in an effort to persuade them to turn to the village station, but complains in the Press that the service is virtually useless.

Much of my own writing is still on railways. The performance in periods of bad weather and on summer Saturdays when four or five times the usual number of expresses trundle down the main line is the subject of perennial interest; one day I might visit Dainton Tunnel to see a new type of diesel on test, the next travel by an enthusiasts' special headed by a veteran steam locomotive; branch line 'funerals' have to be attended, those ambivalent occasions of crowds and cameras and of cries for preservation vitiated by the knowledge that many of the most vociferous passengers are taking their first as well as their final trip. The study of rural transport has brought me to railway problems in other parts of the country. The young firm of David & Charles (Publishers) Limited, run jointly with Charles Hadfield, revolves largely round railway matters. Even while pruning trees on my fruit farm, railways are there, the times of distant trains recorded automatically; nights are occasionally interrupted by tell-tale grunts from a locomotive at odds with Dainton Bank.

And still an enjoyable way of spending a lazy afternoon is to sit beside the railway somewhere between Dainton and Starcross, even if delight at seeing a 13-coach express from Manchester is mingled with sorrow at its lateness, dirtiness or lack of passengers; and holidays to 'get away from it all' bring lengthy train journeys, usually to the Scottish Highlands. It is, of course, the office work that must be escaped from. Railways are taken for granted, permeating work and pleasure. The affinity with them is natural, definitely not a cult, as I think will be found with most seasoned enthusiasts.

An enthusiast could perhaps be loosely described as someone who sees more in railways than a means of transportation. Many of the best railwaymen are not railway enthusiasts, for their interest ceases when they reach home. On holiday they forget trains as I forget writing and farming. The complete enthusiast finds that his love of railways makes him a different man almost as religious convictions might. The change is fundamental.

There is no tidy explanation, but there are probably two main reasons. Firstly, railways are a world of their own; they are segregated from the rest of the nation, and yet they serve it. They are self-contained, definable, understandable even by attentive amateurs and therefore welcoming to escapists; yet they are ubiquitous, infinitely diverse, complex within their own limits and wrapped in their own mystique. They have their own language, their own telephone network, their eating houses, factories and estates; they have their own slums, palaces, mausoleums and rustic beauty; they offer majesty and meanness, laughter, wonder and tears.

Secondly there is the mechanical interest, or to be precise the combination of mechanics and æsthetics, especially in the locomotive and more particularly, of course, the steam engine. Other people have written at length about the appeal of steam, but it can scarcely be over-stated. 'I've been born again since following steam,' a successful motor engineer told me.

99

'It's out of this world.' Steam *is* unique among things mechanical. The love of it is many-sided. My own particular fascination is the relationship between man and machine; others find steam too animate to care about the role of mere humans.

Even my son, aged three, has decided that steam engines are Superior Things, excitement bubbling twice as long after the white clouds have thinned as after the last throb from a diesel, for which he sometimes consoles himself by providing the missing puff. Will he take railway enthusiasm into a third and steamless generation?

I hope that my particular brand of enthusiasm, and especially the excursions into byways, may be enjoyed by others of like tastes. Should any of the uninitiated pursue these pages, perhaps they might find at least a partial understanding of why one person finds railways half a way of life.

A SIGNAL SUCCESS

During the freeze-up in the South West, for the first time for many years I found myself a passenger on the branch line whose every inch I knew as a boy. Memories crowded in as the steam engine alternately struggled up and raced down the inclines on the switchback route, and as the single line 'tokens' were exchanged at signalboxes together with current gossip. But what made me especially nostalgic was a glimpse of the cattle and sheep pens at the country station where I filled in spare hours. The pens were used for the last time just before Christmas, this being among the 2,000 or so stations which British Railways have just closed for livestock traffic; but I shall always picture them as they used to be on fair days and the monthly Great Market day.

An evacuee to the market town in the middle of the 1939-45

war, I made few friends of my own age but was readily accepted as unofficial assistant by the railway staff. After serving an 'apprenticeship' in the goods and parcels office, I graduated to the booking office and signalbox, and was eventually allowed the complete freedom of the station from its warehouses to its water tower—except when officials from district headquarters made their infrequent visits.

My 'duties' were varied. I punched and sorted tickets, made tea, wheeled the platform barrow, coaxed calves out of the guard's van, closed doors, told passengers in the nearby public house when their trains were near, exchanged 'tokens' with the fireman (cider and other provisions for an adjoining remote station were also placed in his custody), and under a watchful eye signalled the engine of the daily 'rabbit special' —up to 30 tons of rabbits nightly—from one end of the two vans to the other. All this was enjoyable enough. The only trouble was the infrequency of the trains. Apart from the rabbit special, which terminated light and started full from our station, on ordinary days there were only five passenger and three goods trains each way, spread out from 5.0 a.m. until 11.0 p.m.

In the long gaps between, all the staff disappeared on fishing, rabbiting, gardening and other expeditions. I read the rule books, picked wild strawberries, eavesdropped on conversations on the 'omnibus' telephone circuit linking all signalboxes on the branch, answered the public telephone (my off-the-cuff knowledge of the timetable became a legend), informed my mother that the town's fortnightly allocation of sausages had come, and served people calling for parcels. (In 1943, a sprinkling of farmers were unable to sign their names and placed a cross or other mark in the register.) But these were no substitute for trains, steam, whistles, 'token' exchanging, lever pulling.

The really worthwhile days, when nothing could prevent me being on 'duty', were summer Saturdays (even in the war extra trains were run to the Atlantic resorts and we boasted

one express), days with troop and other specials (I once signalled General Eisenhower), and above all fair and Great
Market days. These last were the climax of the station's life.

It would all begin a week or so ahead, when the stationmaster came to the signalbox to telephone an order to Control
for a special train of 20 or 25 cattle trucks. The number was
always controversial; we ordered more than we needed and
were sent fewer. Then the timing of the special would be
published in the duplicated announcements of train arrangements circulated to all stations. I was proud to see us figure
with Paddington, Bristol and Plymouth.

The passenger trains brought fair-sized crowds on these
fair and Great Market days, and many found the station a
convenient headquarters, using it for resting, eating, toilet,
telephone, Black Market and other purposes. The empty
cattle special arrived simultaneously with a passenger train in
the other direction while the daily mixed goods was still
shunting in the yard. For me there was the delightful knowledge that we should not be without a train until the cattle
special left four or five hours later, and meanwhile all except
the two distant-signal levers would have to be pulled at least
once.

As I gained experience, the signalman delegated more of
his job, sometimes leaving me—then aged 15—in charge of
the box for short periods while he entered up an accumula-
tion of parcels in the ledger. Then came the day when he
placed me in full control while he assisted in loading a particularly large number of sheep from the pens a considerable
distance away.

The down passenger train was late, that glowing summer
evening, and unable to 'cross' the up train at the usual
station: passing loops are provided at the stations on the
single-track branch. Arrangements therefore had to be changed
on the telephone. In the excitement of being in sole command, I misunderstood the position of the late train, and
reported it wrongly to the next station. Thus instead of let-

ting it go on to this other station, it was decided to 'cross' it at mine.

The train pulled cautiously into the platform, the signal ahead being at danger, but after a few minutes, with still no sign of the up train, it became clear to the staff that something was amiss. The signalman returned, too late to rectify the mistake, but early enough to explain it. Never has my morale been so low as when he told the engine driver that he should have been signalled to the next station to make the 'cross'. At the moment I was not capable of realising the happy potentialities of my lapse.

The guard had more presence of mind.

The train was particularly full, the 150 or so passengers in the three coaches including a party of East End parents going to spend their first week-end with their children who had been evacuated following the first V1 raid on London. After a long, unfamiliar journey, they were not in the best of tempers. Summoning courage, the guard explained that there had been a technical hitch and that they might as well enjoy their wait: they could stretch their legs; there was even time to pop into the pub.

In a second the train was empty. A few went to the pub, but most basked in the evening sunshine, leaning on the railings, gazing at the fields, cattle and sheep. For some it was the first puff of country air ever breathed. Two rabbits scampering in and out of the drain pipes stored in the field at the bottom of the embankment sent a thrill through the whole load. Children squeezed through the railings to pick wild flowers. Never was a station platform so full and yet so peaceful. The only noise came from the cows waiting to be milked—and momentarily from the one disgruntled passenger, a major annoyed at a lively dog entwining his lead around him. To my relief, even the signalman was beaming.

After a lull of 20 or 25 minutes, the signal dropped, passengers climbed aboard, and the train resumed its way. 'Thank you so much. That's been wonderful,' shouted a woman leaning out of the window. I wonder how many remember their country break.

I did not alight at this station the other day, and hope I may never do so before its total closure, which must now be taken for granted. So much has been lost since then: passenger trains carry only a fraction of their former loads, goods trains no longer include the 'station truck' for miscellaneous small items, the station bus service, the rabbit special, even the public house have gone, and now there will be no more cattle specials, or even odd trucks of cattle to be shunted off the last down passenger train by the light of an oil lamp. But worse than this, the staff must now be depressed, bewildered. There could not have been a finer or more loyal lot of men when I knew them, but it is hard to remain loyal to a dying cause, especially if you feel that Authority has a vested interest in its death.

A CORNISH BYWAY

Travelling by train, for most people, involves queueing for tickets, standing on crowded platforms, buying 4d cups of tea, and searching compartments for corner seats. When, however, I decided to go for a journey one recent spare day, I wanted to get away from crowds. So I chose the least-known railway byway in Cornwall. As there have never been passenger trains up the valley of the Camel from Bodmin to Wenford Bridge, there was nothing for it but to use the daily freighter.

I signed a form stating that I would not hold the Transport Commission responsible for the loss of my life, and one dull November morning presented myself at Bodmin General station. British Railways, anxious to please, stopped the Wadebridge train specially for me to alight at Boscarne Junction, and all was set for an unusual journey.

The history of this branch, trying to climb Bodmin Moor and then suddenly giving up the effort, goes back 119 years. On 13 October 1834 the Bodmin & Wadebridge Railway (the first in the Westcountry to be worked by locomotives) opened its 'main' line between Wadebridge and Wenford Bridge. Great was the excitement when the 'very beautiful and powerful engine was put in motion, and it proceeded drawing the long train of carriages amidst the cheers of the multitudes'.

'The wagons,' we are told, 'were tastefully fitted up with flags and evergreens, one flag displaying the words: "Science, Prudence, and Perseverance". The Royal Cornwall Militia played the National Anthem. The scene defies description: a more grand and imposing sight was never perhaps witnessed in this county.' The first train ran all the way from Wadebridge to Wenford Bridge, some 12 miles. Soon, however, the Bodmin 'branch' became the main line, and so far as I know the seven miles from Boscarne Junction to Wenford Bridge were never again the centre of public attention. For four generations goods traffic has trundled its course undisturbed.

And now back to the daily goods train. It left Wadebridge at 10.3 a.m., and at 10.50 we said farewell to Boscarne Junction and civilisation. To emphasise our isolation the travelling shunter closed the gate across the track behind us.

We moved a few yards and stopped. The shunter alighted again, and with a red flag halted traffic on the main Bodmin—Wadebridge road while we crossed it on the level. Only one engine is allowed on the branch at a time, says the rule book, 'and as the branch is not provided with signals, fencing, or any protection, the train passing over it must be moved at such speed as it can be stopped promptly before reaching any obstruction that may be observed on the line by the engine-man'. No traffic is allowed after dark, but in summer up to three separate trips may be made daily. This time our load was 22 empty clay wagons.

The procession stopped in a delightfully sylvan setting beside the River Camel at Penhargard, and the fireman climbed on to a primitive water tower to give the engine a drink. Water is put in the tank by the simple expedient of running it by gravity from a stream higher up the valley.

As I explained, the last time the line was in the public eye was 119 years ago. A passenger (especially a reporter) was regarded as a bit of a novelty. 'What made you want to come up here?' enquired Driver Tucker. The Wenford 'run' is given to the oldest driver at Wadebridge. 'A nice quiet job,' he said. A nice quiet job, too, for the engine: herself almost older than living memory. Built by the London & South Western Railway engineer Beattie, No. 30585, this remarkable 2—4—0 tank engine is a piece of history. She began her career as a main-line express engine in the 1870s, but in 1895 was relegated to branch work. She (and two of her kindred stationed at Wadebridge) have been retained because the curves on the branch (and in Wadebridge yard) are so sharp that no other engine will round them.

The line follows the beautiful but little-known Camel River. Views from the track are grand. Once the Southern Railway thought of running a passenger service, but the experimental coach stuck on a curve and had to be pulled off. The scenery is enhanced by the avenues of oak trees planted by the lineside by the Bodmin & Wadebridge company; but oaks have their disadvantage. Frequently the staff have difficulty in clearing the track of pigs searching for acorns.

A mile or so after our halt for water, we stopped at Helland Bridge and exchanged a friendly greeting with Mr Charles Marshall. Aged 85, he has lived in Railway Cottage since he was five months old. He still performs the duties of wharfinger —old terms die hard—to the railway, for which he gets his home rent-free. His mother and father had the job before him. Mrs Edith Smith has for 25 years performed similar duties at Tresarrett—in the siding is a truck of feeding stuffs for the local mill. Her husband is one of three men who spend their time looking after the permanent way. Railway work traditionally goes in families. Our driver was one of five brothers who passed their lives in the service of the Southern Railway, and his father and mother were also railway employees.

As we continued on our journey with a gentle chuff we threw out copies of the day's paper—an unofficial delivery service for outlying farms. Then, 6½ miles from Boscarne (accomplished in one hour 12 minutes, during which our conversation had put the universe right), we stopped at the china-clay works which provides the branch with much of its

LAUNCESTON BRANCH. Top: 5569 on 2.5 p.m. Launceston to Plymouth parallels the Southern line with Brentor in the background in August 1962. Middle: Mist lies over the Lower Plym valley as 0—6—0 No. 6430, leaving a trail of exhaust in the frosty air, hurries past Plym Bridge Platform on the 11.10 a.m. S.O. Plymouth—Tavistock on 22 December 1962, a week before final closure. Bottom: 6430 leaves Marsh Mills with the 2.10 p.m. Plymouth to Tavistock as the snow starts to thicken on closing night, 29 December 1962

WEST COUNTRY NOTEBOOK (see page 185). Top: *T9 at Saltash passage in 1959*. Middle left: *The restored T9 No. 120 on 'North Cornishman' at Okehampton in April 1963*. Middle right: *'Penlee'— before receiving its name—on the Newlyn quarry railway at the turn of the century*. Bottom: *Teetotal gala excursion crossing Redruth viaduct in 1851*

traffic. Here the crew spent a busy hour shunting, replacing empty clay wagons with full ones of 'white gold' for shipment at Fowey. At the end of the hour, Driver Tucker carefully opened the regulator of his veteran locomotive and we proceeded to the terminus at Wenford Bridge, where granite is the chief traffic. Once an inclined plane ran up to the de Lank quarries, but now the famous Cornish granite is brought to the station by road.

'True, it's a bit quiet up here,' said the station clerk, Mr Pethick, 'but according to a cutting I have, it seems there was a plan to use this route to take traffic from Ireland to London.' It sounds an odd idea, but in 1863 it was proposed to extend the railway from Wenford Bridge to Launceston, which, said Mr Pethick's cutting, 'would open up a large district of development. With the proposed harbour of refuge on the North Cornish coast, this railway would provide a new and shorter route from Cork to London.'

A hundred and nineteen years is a good score for any railway. How many more years will be added to the life of the Wenford Bridge line? The prospects are good. We returned to civilisation with a full load of granite and china clay.

*   *   *

Just discovered in an old loft near Wadebridge are documents, letters, account books and journals which have lain quietly in the dust for several generations. They answer many questions about the pioneer Bodmin & Wadebridge Railway which have long puzzled railway enthusiasts and historians.

The Bodmin & Wadebridge was opened only four years after the Liverpool & Manchester Railway and became famous because of its early coach designs. Some coaches are still preserved—though not, alas, in Cornwall.

In every respect it was unusual. Passengers were carried only on certain days of the week, but the company was not without initiative. On 13 April 1834 a 'special' conveyed the people of Wadebridge to Bodmin to witness the execution of two murderers—an edifying spectacle which they may have

111

seen comfortably while seated in the train on the line near the old prison. It appears that other specials could be ordered at short notice. A letter in the collection reads: 'We shall have a party of 40 to take to Grogley tomorrow and we shall expect train at 8.0. If wet morning it would be useless to go, so please

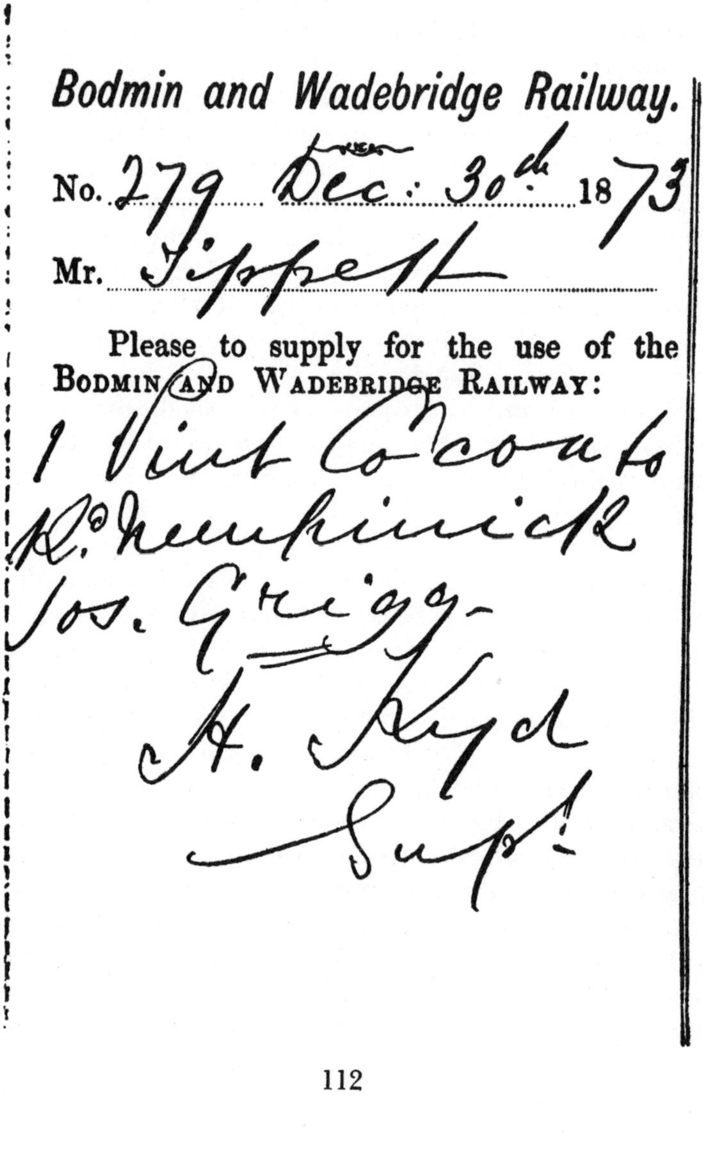

Bodmin and Wadebridge Railway.

No. 279   Dec: 30th   18 73

Mr. Tippett

Please to supply for the use of the BODMIN AND WADEBRIDGE RAILWAY:

1 Pint Cocoa to
R. Newkirk
Jos. Grigg

H. Kyd
Supt

don't send train. Will take children to Dunmere in the afternoon instead, where we could walk.'

Normally one afternoon and one evening train ran each
way between Bodmin and Wadebridge. Passengers were
warned of starting time by blasts on the engine whistle given
ten, five and one minute before departure. Trains could be
halted when required. One gentleman wrote to the superintendent thanking the staff for their 'very courteous attention
when the train turned back when I accidentally dropped my
purse out'. An early railway enthusiast asked the superintendent, H. Kyd, for pictures of the first two engines, *Camel* and
Elephant. Mr Kyd was not to be bothered with that nonsense
and wrote on the envelope 'not answered'.

Among the documents is an extraordinarily large number
of slips ordering pints of cocoa for the employees. The whole
staff seems to have lived on cocoa, and the establishments
which supplied it must have thrived. There are also quantities
of pay sheets. While at one time bargemen (who brought
Camel estuary sand to Wadebridge for the railway to convey
inland) were paid 3s a tide and casual labourers received 14s
a week. The top weekly wage in the locomotive department
was 30s.

Perhaps the most interesting of the records is the first 'Day
Book' kept in the copperplate writing of Mr Kyd. It starts on
4 July 1834 with the entry: 'The engine was tried first time.'
That was *Camel*. On 30 September: 'According to Notice the
Road was this day Publicly opened.' On 15 October: 'In
returning the axle of Feeder broke.' The next day: 'On
starting the axle broke again.'

On 15 January 1835: 'One pair of wheels of the Engine
injured by repeatedly getting between the Rails, obliged to
stop.' On 19 January: 'Attempted to get steam, but the pipes
leaking so badly were unable to do so; so took out fire.' On
23 January: 'Broke off the Chimney of the Engine.' What an
engine! February 14: 'Found the Engine leaking so much as
to oblige her to be stopped for repair.' Four days later: 'Gave

up the attempt to work Engine and proceeded to take it to pieces by Order of the Directors.' Not until 15 April was the machine out again. In June the wheels gave trouble. 2 June: 'Changing a pair of Wheels to the Engine.' 17 June: 'Engine wheels became crippled, obliged to stop.' And so on. Wheels continued to be damaged as soon as they were changed, and horses had to maintain the important sand traffic inland and granite traffic back to Wadebridge. 31 July: 'Left at Junction IX wagons of sand in consequence of a wheel of Engine failing.' On 16 October comes the revealing entry: 'Stopped the Engine in consequence of the wheels being of different sizes, which shook the whole so much as to break a Spring.'

On 17 May 1836 *Elephant* arrived on the schooner *Sophia* at Wadebridge (then a flourishing port) to help the hard-pressed Camel. In a few days she was ready for service: 'The Elephant with omnibus cab and 17 wagons proceeded over the whole line with Passengers. The Camel followed the Elephant with 14 wagons supposed to have taken 800 persons. Received on account of passengers, £25 1s 0d at 1s each.' Next week the newcomer was in trouble: 'Several pieces of granite fell off the wagon which occasioned much delay and consumption in steam which caused the lead rivet to melt. Obliged to take out the fire and bring Engine home with Cattle.'

The weather's influence was profound. On 2 February 1836: 'Snow on the ground. Found it unprofitable to work.' On 28 November: 'P.M. About 3 got Elephant out of the house. Proceeded with Truck of coal and VIII of sand intended for Nanstallen. When at the Bridge under Pendovey, the weather being very rough and the evening very dark, found it necessary to return.' In May next year the engines were 'unemployed fearing the consequences of the dry weather'.

It should not be thought that the railway was always at a standstill. On 14 June 1837: 'At 5 o'clock the Camel left for Wenford, at 7 the Elephant for Bodmin. At 10.15 both

Engines returned. At 11 the two Engines with 27 vehicles left for the head of the line, carrying about 400 passengers. At 7.30 the Camel returned. At 10 the Elephant returned. No accident of any kind occurred during the day. Amount of passengers booked £26 11s 6d.' The next day's entry is significant: 'Engines not working.'

For 54 years the Bodmin & Wadebridge remained an isolated concern: what had seemed go-ahead in 1834 must have appeared antiquated when a connection was made with the Great Western outside Bodmin. In 1845 the railway was bought by the London & South Western. The LSWR was still 200 miles away and the purchase was illegal, but it was largely this astute move which led to the GWR being kept off the Atlantic coast from Minehead to Newquay.

(*Pictures page 92*)

FAREWELL TO SEAGOOD

This is about a railway that was forced to close because it became too popular. The management could not cope and, rather than favour some travellers to the exclusion of others, the directors called in the receiver.

It happened like this. Just before the war, my family moved from London to Devon. We were warned by our friends that we should be cutting ourselves off from civilisation, but this was a prospect which pleased my father, who among other things looked forward to greater leisure for building and running the Paddington to Seagood model railway.*

For a while all went well. We laid out our model on benches in a room 27 by 19½ feet and, with four stations and 12 Great Western engines, in our quiet way we entertained ourselves by running trains. We put the emphasis on the life-like performance of every movement, and certainly with our 'King' and 'Castle' and our scale coaches with glass windows and interior seats and tables, the railway was no mere toy.

* Described on page 78

Local residents, however, soon took a different view. Mothers looked upon our 'train set' as an obvious source of amusement for the children. 'Would you mind if I brought John and Mary along to see your little railway?' was the all-too-frequent request on the telephone, and on wet afternoons toward the end of the school holidays carloads of children would be dumped at our front door without warning.

By now the railway had been the subject of articles and pictures in the Press. Our London friends heard of it and made it the excuse to visit us—we saw more of them in our first summer in Devon than during the previous five years. Railway enthusiasts from all over Britain and the Empire arrived, singly and in parties.

The least popular callers were naturally those who had used the railway merely as a lever to gain entry—people who dismissed the model in a single glance, and with their back to the *Cornish Riviera Express* talked solidly of politics or their aches and pains. A few appreciated the realism of the system so little that they romped about, gave children pick-a-backs and lounged across the track of the main line.

Visitors genuinely interested were almost exclusively men: professors, politicians, parsons and porters met on equal terms. Real engine drivers asked if they might start the locomotive hauling the *Devonian,* while managing directors acted as shunters. 'Could I see your model railway?' asked a voice on the telephone. An hour later, not one man but nine arrived—members of a model club on an outing, including a lawyer, a dentist, a motor mechanic and a real railway signalman. Only after we glanced at the visitors' book after he had left did we realise that one day we entertained a very distinguished guest: we had been too absorbed by the trains to ask personal questions during his stay. Our best-remembered visitor was the Army private who said that studying a plan of our layout published in the *Model Railway News* had been his sole means of preserving sanity during a 'fairly nasty' period on the beach at Dunkirk.

Two terminus stations on branches and two intermediate stations on the continuous double-track main line made up our system. The larger terminus was of course Paddington, the smaller Seagood—a fictitious name for the dreamlike holiday resort the railway served. Though stopping at Taunton, Exeter and Newton Abbot and carrying miniature destination boards labelled Penzance, all trains ended their journeys at Seagood. Imaginary Seagood, especially in relation to Paddington, had an important psychological effect. Trains reached Newton Abbot punctually, but after the customary long wait there, they entered the land where time was of less importance. In fact it was always noon at that perfect holiday resort by the emerald sea. Even the eyes of hard-headed Birmingham businessmen watered when 0—4—0 *Skylark* pulled into Seagood's dead end. 'Seagood for the holidays' was our slogan.

We certainly saw a cross-section of humanity in our railway room. We met fascinating people, and undoubtedly gave pleasure to many. But the telephone and the doorbell rang too often . . . and an Englishman's home is his castle. Total closure seemed less painful than rejecting all visitors, or discriminating between would-be callers.

The last train scheduled never ran. Its engine, *Pendennis Castle*, broke down—the first failure we had had for years. Rolling stock and stations have been sent to buyers all over Britain. We have just finished cutting up the benches. But we still cherish the warm dream of Seagood.

NARROW GAUGE TO KILLYBEGS

One of my most prized possessions is a ticket issued to my wife and me by the County Donegal Railways Joint Committee. It reads: 'PASS Mr. and Mrs. Thomas TO all stations FROM all stations AND BACK'. Alas, during a short tour of Ireland to study transport problems we had little time to take advantage of this magical document, and to my lasting regret I was unable to accept the offer of a footplate ride through the Barnesmore Gap.

We did, however, travel down the main line from Strabane to Killybegs and back, and it was during this journey that the idea of a book on the system was born. The railway immediately struck me, a dispassionate observer, as a remarkable enterprise. The first surprise, of course, was that there should be a narrow-gauge railway at all in so thinly-peopled an area as late as the mid-1950s. Merely to travel on the trains seemed to be stepping back in history. But any thoughts of their being a mere quaint anachronism were rapidly dispelled. Until the end, the railway played a vital part in the life of the community it served, and it was run with exemplary efficiency.

Above all, the system impressed me with its friendliness. Here were none of the formalities and none of the dignity which so often seem designed to reduce the stature of passengers on standard-gauge railways. The County Donegal Railways were simple, domesticated—no impersonal organisation sheltering behind a mystique. Relations between staff and passengers, and among the staff themselves, were eminently human. Another attractive feature was the railway's unself-consciousness; being so far removed from big centres it was relatively little visited by enthusiasts. There was no temptation to become a show or museum piece: the local population always came first.

Although my visit was short, I came away with many memories to cherish. Some of these centre on the enthusiastic welcome given me at the Stranorlar headquarters, with its loco and carriage shops, its sweet-stall in the booking hall, its diminutive footbridge and its incongruous clock-tower above the gentlemen's lavatory. The coaches stabled in the bay platform pending the departure of the next steam-hauled excursion were unlocked for examination, and the railcars were run out from the maintenance shed especially for me to photograph them. On departure, I sat beside the driver for the journey on to Killybegs. The grim grandeur of the Barnesmore Gap was impressive enough, but what most excited me was the last section, along the rough, tortuous and quite undeveloped Atlantic seaboard. The diesel horn echoed: the crossing keepers opened the gates; mothers and children rushed to the doorways of the whitewashed crossing cottages; and labourers digging tiny patches of peaty soil at the cliff's edge set their watches as we rollicked by. The driver apologised for the rough riding: I should have come when the track was as good as anything I would have seen in England, he said. Talking about England, 'My daddy once went there. I've never been myself, of course.' And so into the dilapidated little port of Killybegs, where the most modern object was an oil tank wagon, a neat miniature of Esso's British wagons, standing in the siding.

Here was a service worth recording.

(Pictures pages 145 and 174)

121

THE C.K. & P.

The study of the cross-country line from Penrith through Keswick to Workington was an important feature of the Lake District Transport Enquiry (of which the author was director).

Most of the survey work was undertaken in summer 1960, when British Railways were known to be considering the possibility of withdrawing passenger trains. In October an interim report of our findings was presented to the North Western Transport Users' Consultative Committee. Almost simultaneously, British Railways announced a reprieve of passenger services 'at least for the time being', and a conference of the Press and representatives of local organisations was later called by railway officials at Penrith. At this meeting, and also at an earlier meeting of the Enquiry's Steering Committee, British Railways largely agreed with the findings of the interim report, which estimated an annual loss of £50,000 on the line.

The railway is $39\frac{3}{4}$ miles long. (As a useful comparison,

Workington to Penrith is further than Paddington to Reading, and Keswick to Carlisle just as far.) About $13\frac{1}{2}$ miles (Penruddock to Threlkeld, and Brigham to Derwent Junction, near Workington, where the branch joins the Coastal line) is double track, a legacy of the days when substantial freight traffic used the route on its way from the east to the west coast. Gradients are severe, with several sections at 1 in 70, and a bank of four miles at 1 in 63 between Threlkeld and Troutbeck.

In the past the western end of the branch had substantial local passenger traffic: Brigham and Cockermouth were both junctions for other passenger services, and between Workington and Cockermouth several of the intermediate stations now closed were once important enough for trains to terminate and start there. Although the last purely local train between Workington and Cockermouth survived the war, today nearly all local passengers between the two places go by road, and passenger traffic is heavier at the eastern end of the line, between Keswick and Penrith. But all weekday trains travel right through from Penrith to Workington and *vice-versa*.

All the branch lines formerly connecting with this railway are closed even to goods, and there is no remnant of the once-substantial coal traffic at the western end. But freight is still heavier here than at the eastern end, Cockermouth being the distribution point for a range of goods, including oil, over a wide area.

The line was among the first in Britain to benefit from the introduction of diesel multiple-unit trains. These arrived in February 1955, when the service was appreciably increased and accelerated. Blencow station, which had previously closed, was reopened and remains open. But another intermediate station served by the diesels for several years has since closed: Embleton, between Bassenthwaite Lake and Cockermouth. There are now nine intermediate stations between Penrith and Workington, of which Keswick and Cockermouth are obviously the most important.

Another improvement introduced with dieselisation was the running of a number of through trains to and from Carlisle (*via* Penrith). Also, since 1955 the line, which for many years had run on weekdays only, has had a Sunday service in summer. Connections at Workington for Whitehaven have generally worsened since dieselisation, however.

The basic weekday train service consists of eight diesels in each direction. During the summer, though not for the whole duration of the summer timetable, there is in addition a steam-hauled section of the *Lakes Express*, with through coaches to and from London; and on summer Saturdays a through service runs to and from Manchester. On summer Sundays there is a skeleton service of diesels and a steam train—the only one of the week with restaurant facilities—from Newcastle; on about half the Sundays during the season a special excursion runs from such places as Morecambe and Blackpool. On the freight side, daily trains run from Penrith to Keswick and back, and from Workington to Keswick and back. There is an additional early-morning freight and parcels train from Penrith to Keswick: the locomotive works back light to Blencow, where it shunts in the limestone-quarry sidings.

We estimated that on Mondays to Fridays in September the total number of passengers at all intermediate stations, joining or alighting from the eight trains in each direction, averaged about 350 a day, and in winter little if any above 200 a day, or less than $1\frac{1}{2}$ per stop. On many days the average would be less than one person per booked stop. Though certain trains could run non-stop from Penrith to Keswick without inconveniencing anyone, other services draw a high proportion of their small total of passengers from intermediate stations.

In view of the paucity of traffic, the question is: what inconvenience would the withdrawal of trains cause?

Local patronage. The majority of local passengers would be able to travel by road without much hardship, though many journeys would take longer and cost more. Careful examination of the traffic suggested that if the railway closed only about one-third of the journeys would be made by bus instead of train. One-third would be made by private motor vehicle, and the remaining third would cease. Visits to Carlisle would be especially reduced.

Long-distance travellers. Less than 20 per cent of Keswick's visitors arrive by train; of those who now do so, a considerable proportion would probably go elsewhere (mainly still within the Lake District) upon the closure of the branch. It was noted here as elsewhere in the Lake District that young people travelling long distances still mostly use trains. It is well known that older people return to scenes of earlier holidays at least occasionally. If, lacking a railway, fewer new visitors are introduced to Keswick and district, it is reasonable to suppose that the supply of 'regulars' and 'semi-regulars' in future years will also suffer. As an incidental, the withdrawal of trains would almost certainly end the Keswick Convention.

From the point of view of the local economy, the railway's long-distance traffic may well be of greater importance than its scale suggests, though of course it might be a matter of indifference to British Railways that the closure of the branch now would result in Keswick receiving fewer motoring visitors in years to come.

The local population would also miss the railway connections with long-distance trains at Penrith and Carlisle, and cars and taxis would have to be used more often. The Transport Commission's present policy is against running a special service of buses for railway needs, and the adaptation of the existing bus service to give main-line connections at Penrith would not be satisfactory.

Excursionists. In summer the majority of passengers are apt to be holidaymakers on day excursions. The elimination of one or more possible trips from the Lakeland itinerary would cause them no hardship, but the line is part of the Lakeland scene and visitors would regret its loss: it is now used by many on 'round trips' up the Shap line to Penrith and down the Coastal line *via* Workington and Barrow. But most holidaymakers staying in Keswick use trains only for short journeys, and in the whole of August 1960 only 64 runabout tickets were sold at Keswick.

Parcels and freight traffic. Keswick's isolation would preclude any economic road service from equalling the present good passenger-train deliveries of newspapers and parcels. The withdrawal of freight facilities would, however, cause relatively little inconvenience. Deliveries of some goods would be delayed, road congestion would be slightly worse, and the price of coal might rise, but industries would not suffer seriously. Complete closure of the branch between Cockermouth and Blencow could be economically better justified than closure to passengers only. Penrith—Blencow would have to be kept for limestone traffic, and there would be a strong case for retaining Workington—Cockermouth for general freight. This would leave $12\frac{3}{4}$ miles of the present $39\frac{3}{4}$ miles.

If this line serves definite passenger needs, with good parcels and freight facilities, how could the results be improved? What economies could be made?

Train service. Some trains are almost always well used while others, particularly at midday and at the western end of the branch, are nearly empty, summer and winter alike. It is suggested that the standard weekday service could be reduced to seven trains in each direction between Penrith and Keswick, and to four or five beyond. A summary of suggestions for bringing the service more into line with traffic demands has been submitted to British Railways.

Singling of track. Even with the present service there is no justification for retaining the $13\frac{1}{2}$ miles of double track.

Signalling. Again, even supposing the present train service was maintained, signalling costs could be materially cut. The suggestions below take into account the proposed reduction in train service. Five signalboxes could be closed, saving at least £7,500 a year. *Brigham*: to become 'crossing' station between

STEAM'S INDIAN SUMMER. Top: *O. V. S. Bulleid*. Middle and bottom: *'Elder Dempster' as originally built and as rebuilt*

BULLEID PACIFICS. Top: *Rebuilt 'Merchant Navy' No. 35029 tops the summit of Buckhorn Weston Tunnel in October 1961 with the up 'Atlantic Coast Express'.* Bottom: *Un-rebuilt 'West Country' No. 43043 near Wincanton on the Somerset & Dorset line with the down 'Pines Express' in August 1962*

two single-track sections. There is an important level crossing here. *Cockermouth*: signalbox to be closed and only one platform of passenger station to be used. Access to goods yards at passenger station to be by use of key in the single-line electric token apparatus. This would repeat the arrangement already introduced at Cockermouth main goods yard some distance away. *Embleton*: signalbox to be closed and level crossing to become the responsibility of crossing keeper living in station house. *Bassenthwaite Lake*: signalbox to be maintained as at present; there is a level crossing here. The shortening of the loop line would enable signalman to command all movements himself without assistance of a porter. *Braithwaite*: signalbox to be abolished as intermediate block post, and level crossing to become a porter's responsibility. *Keswick*: one of the two signalboxes to be closed. *Threlkeld*: at present the track becomes double here; when it is singled a section from Keswick to Troutbeck is proposed, Threlkeld box being closed. *Troutbeck*: this would become a crossing station, and the signalbox, now open only when required, would be regularly operated. *Penruddock*: at present the double track becomes single here. It is suggested that Troutbeck—Blencow should be one section when track is singled, and the signalbox here closed. *Blencow*: to remain as at present.

Some signalling economies would have been possible years ago. The signalbox at Cockermouth Junction was abolished only recently, but could well have gone before the war. Embleton station was closed in 1958, but all trains still have virtually to stop there to exchange the electric token with the signalman, much to the annoyance of local people who claim that they have been inconvenienced while little if any expense has been saved: a signalbox is not needed, and British Railways now intend appointing a crossing keeper instead. At Keswick, expenditure of a few hundred pounds would have enabled one of the two signalboxes to have closed 25 or more years ago.

Unstaffed halts. Retaining staff for platform duties at most of the small stations seems entirely unjustified. On the other hand, some trains regularly pick up or set down workers, schoolchildren or shoppers at all stations: while the stations are there and the diesels, capable of rapid acceleration, are passing them it would seem foolish to prevent such passengers travelling, or indeed to inflict the loss of traffic upon the railway itself. It is strongly urged that most of the small stations should become unstaffed halts, and that the number of trains stopping there should be reduced in the light of experience. Probably about £4,000 annually could be saved by reducing station staffs.

The suggestion most frequently met was that traffic could easily be vastly increased. We do not accept this. Populations are small, and the average length of even local journeys is necessarily long, with substantial fares. An increasing number of people will travel by car whatever the train service, and the western end of the branch faces competition from a good bus service.

But certainly a number of things could be done. As against the economies that have been suggested, a small expenditure might be considered on improving connections at Workington for Whitehaven and the Coastal line. For some years it has been near-impossible to travel from Keswick to Ravenglass for the Eskdale Railway and back in time for hotel dinner; running the second down train of the day rather earlier would provide a valuable connection. Then, at present the *Lakes Express* runs three weeks less than the summer timetable period, but runs on the three Saturdays concerned: to retain it for the remaining 15 days would usefully simplify the timetable and cost comparatively little.

Publicity could be improved. Most Keswick hotels had details of coach but not of railway tours. In January 1961 the only railway notice board in the town (at the bus station) had a torn timetable. Many local people travel by train to Carlisle on market day, the trip being cheap and quick, but no effort is made to advertise to visitors the train's advantage.

A good case can be made for retaining the line, primarily to benefit the local economy, though also for the well-being of British Railways themselves. Closure would result in much through traffic taking to the road the whole way, and fewer runabout tickets would be sold. Keswick is the capital of the Northern Lakes, and to withdraw trains would, to a much greater extent than most closures, give the impression that the railways are dying.

It is estimated that the proposals made above could result in cutting the annual loss from about £50,000 to about £25,000. The loss would remain considerable, but there would be the satisfaction that the money was being better spent. Yet a rapid 'spring clean' seems improbable. Permission has to be obtained from regional headquarters at Euston, which in turn is controlled by the Transport Commission and the Minister of Transport, to spend the small amount of capital needed to effect the annual savings, and everywhere British Railways are short of money for immediate use.

(Pictures page 56)

STEAM'S INDIAN SUMMER

Transport history takes some peculiar turns. It is difficult to produce a more dramatic opening, for my story is necessarily involved. But consider this odd set of circumstances.

The Southern Region has the greatest proportion of electrified track and, like its predecessor the Southern Railway, has always been held to take relatively little interest in steam motive power. But its Waterloo—Exeter route is the last trunk line in Britain to be exclusively steam operated. This might be regarded as mere conservatism, but the fastest trains were accelerated last September (1961), and higher average speeds are now being achieved more regularly than ever before. The down *Atlantic Coast Express*, for example, is allowed 77 minutes for the 75¾ miles of switchback between Salisbury and Sidmouth Junction, where it often arrives early; an average of 65 miles an hour is not infrequent, and averages as high as 82 miles an hour have been recorded over 50-mile sections of the route.

At the same time, the Western Region, upon reaching the long-planned complete dieselisation of Paddington—West expresses, slowed down the fastest services. The *Torbay Express* (admittedly not now the Western's best train) takes longer to reach Exeter over its easier route than does the *Atlantic Coast Express*, and is more often late.

The Southern's success has been made possible by the 'Merchant Navy' class locomotives which have just come of age—the first, *Channel Packet,* was named by Lord Brabazon in the dark days of 1941—and were designed by Mr O. V. S. Bulleid. He is the last of the long line of original and individualistic steam engineers. Now living in retirement at Exmouth, he is acknowledged to be a remarkable designer. But he takes no pride in the present achievements: first, because he thinks that diesels could do better with less expense; and secondly, because the 'Merchant Navy' locomotives have recently been rebuilt, and (especially in outward appearance) are not like those he produced.

The steam locomotive was born in an atmosphere of controversy, and apparently its days must end in similar mood. Although he left the Southern many years ago, Mr Bulleid is more than a little annoyed that the originality of his invention has been spoilt.

The 'Merchant Navy' class was designed for minimum maintenance. Believing it old-fashioned, even degrading, for an engine-driver to have to plod round with an oilcan, Mr Bulleid covered up the 'works' with a streamlined casing. Although the engines embodied many other new features, unrepentantly he holds that the streamlining was the greatest step forward. In the rebuilding, of course, the casing has been removed, leaving a distinctly more traditional appearance.

The cost of rebuilding is said to be about £15,000 apiece—half the cost of the original locomotives. 'I think it's a waste of money,' Mr Bulleid told me. 'If they were not fit to continue in their present form, British Railways should have scrapped them. The money would have been much better spent on fitting them with mechanical stokers earlier on.' One of Mr Bulleid's two regrets was that the fireman could not feed the boiler fast enough to realise the full potential power: but after experiments it was decided not to add mechanical stokers. The other regret was that, in one respect, the design proved almost too good: the drop in pressure from the regulator to the cylinders was so small that drivers found it hard to start without wheels slipping.

After the 'Merchant Navy' class came the similar but lighter 'Battle of Britain' and 'West Country' classes, the latter specially designed to cross Meldon Viaduct near Okehampton, with its severe width and weight restrictions. The arrival of the new streamlined locomotives at Ilfracombe and Wadebridge after the war had an almost magical effect on the 'withered arm', the Southern's system west of Exeter. Hitherto the North Devon and North Cornwall lines had made do with the rest of the system's left-offs, antediluvian in appearance and whistles, albeit Dugald Drummond's 4—4—0 T9s, the 'Greyhounds', of 1899 to 1901 vintage, lived up to their reputation and made many a sprightly run across the central Devon plateauland well into the 1950s.

Mr Bulleid enjoys recalling the favourable local public reaction to the 'West Country' class; but that he is no sentimentalist may be gauged from the fact that he does not possess a single photograph of one of these engines. According to him, in opposition to GWR conviction, a locomotive is purely a piece of machinery. No concession should be made for appearance. Aesthetics do not come into it. And like all machinery, when it grows old it should be scrapped. Mr Bulleid wants none of his engines preserved in museums.

His final design for the Southern was the most controversial of all—the 'Leader' class, of which only the first was built. Outwardly it was more like a diesel than a steam engine. Uncompromisingly ugly, it cost the Southern a considerable amount of goodwill and a great deal of cash before it was cut up for scrap. In some ways, however, it was the best design of all time. Certainly the boiler was the tightest ever placed on the rails.

Mr Bulleid left the Southern to modernise the railways of Coras Iompair Eireann, which under his guidance were dieselised earlier and more rapidly than British Railways. He did not design diesels—to duplicate the specialists' experience would have been pointless—and in fact the only engine he designed after the 'Leader' was a peat-burning one, first of a class the Irish Government, with bitter memories of fuel shortages in the war, planned to build for strategic reasons.

Too late, and yet in some ways too advanced, Mr Bulleid has perhaps never realised his own potential. But he has an assured place in railway history and literature. Perhaps I may be excused for quoting a passage from Mr Hamilton Ellis's *Four Main Lines* which sums up so well his matter-of-fact approach to his machines. Describing a test run behind the prodigy *Channel Packet*, which bore 'not the remotest resemblance to anything else on British or foreign rails', Mr Ellis says:

'We smelt things, the speed dropped, I put away my borrowed stopwatch that formed my luggage, and stuck my head out of the window. Yes, the great engine had come off at Basingstoke. Clouds of smoke seemed to be coming from the box of tricks underneath. People rushed around, looking grave and anxious—except Mr Bulleid himself. May I be forgiven for recording that he looked like a boy with a new and wondrous mechanical toy that had done just what he expected it might, and furnished an excuse for more tinkering?'

(*Pictures pages 127 and 128*)

VITAL BUT NOT VIABLE

Receipts from the conveyance of passengers and goods cover less than half the cost of running North Devon's railway system. Many individual trains and stations do not earn a fifth of their costs. In total the loss on the passenger system works out at £5—£6 per annum per head of the district's population. The transfer of all traffic now carried by train to the roads would make relatively little difference to road congestion.

Yet North Devon's removal from the railway map would cause widespread economic and social hardship. Fewer tourists would visit the resorts; fewer newly-retired people would come to settle in the area; the chances of solving the long-standing unemployment problem would be substantially reduced; and generally North Devon would be placed at a severe disadvantage compared with the rest of Southern England.

North Devon's railways are little used, but they are still essential: that the area is highly dependent upon what could easily be dismissed as a white elephant is a paradox which must be understood clearly, both locally and by the Government, if action which might lead to distress and depopulation is to be avoided.

The first point to be emphasised is that road transport is chosen almost automatically for both passenger and goods journeys to and from, and within North Devon unless there is a specific advantage in using the railways. From this it follows that the majority of people and goods still using trains are doing so because no alternative exists or because the alternative is much slower or more expensive. Research undertaken for this report has produced abundant evidence to support this statement. Not only was it found that people still travelling by train had a particular reason for doing so, but it was possible to tell precisely what that reason was in the majority of cases before actually questioning the people concerned.

Passenger traffic falls into three main categories:

1. Long-distance. The long-distance services and connections are undoubtedly the most important. As will be explained later, the majority of passengers on long-distance train journeys do not regard coach and bus travel as a feasible alternative. Those prepared to go by coach and bus mostly do so already.

2. All-the-year-round local travel. With few exceptions the railways are now carrying only the leavings from the bus services. Thus there is little local traffic on the Taunton—Barnstaple line between Taunton and Wiveliscombe, and between South Molton and Barnstaple, where bus services are good. But the railway still provides the only public transport for a number of villages in the sparsely-populated area in between. In the Taw Valley between Crediton and Barnstaple the more important wayside stations remain relatively busy as there is no bus service. Between Barnstaple and Bideford, and

again between Bideford and Torrington, most local passengers go by bus, but the smaller number making the entire Barnstaple—Torrington journey choose the railway as there is no through bus and connections are poor.

3. Excursion traffic. Cheap tickets, including runabout tickets, entice to the railways some travellers who would otherwise have used a bus. These are the only train travellers who would not be seriously inconvenienced by the closure of the railways *without* the introduction of special bus replacements.

Likewise, the railways' goods traffic is mainly in two categories:

1. Goods which are the natural prerogative of the railways —mail, newspapers and perishables for which there is no road equivalent in speed and regularity, and coal for which the railways are still more effective and cheaper on long-distance hauls.

2. Miscellaneous goods mainly in small consignments for which road transport has not troubled to compete.

The combination of traffic obviously suitable for rail transport (such as long-distance passengers and milk) with traffic obviously unsuitable (such as people going from village to village and the occasional peak-time load from a firm which normally transports all its goods by road) has led to an unhappy compromise.

To quote the most obvious example, because there is no bus service in the Taw Valley, most passenger trains, including those to and from London, stop at up to 11 stations between Exeter and Barnstaple, and every train (except on summer Saturdays) stops at all 12 stations between Taunton and Barnstaple. This has induced many long-distance travellers who value their time to drive to Exeter or Taunton stations. The passenger from London who is met by a car at Taunton can often be in Barnstaple half-an-hour earlier than if he did the whole journey by train. Their Victorian crawl has inevitably depleted the railways' long-distance traffic to North Devon and made it less worthwhile for them to improve their service.

The situation on the goods side is not quite so clear-cut but in the long run could be even more serious. Large merchants with steady business have to a great extent deserted the railways because the train services and charges are geared to smaller, irregular consignments.

In North Devon, more than in most areas, the railways have lost the very type of freight they are now seeking to carry. Conversely they carry much which ultimately they would like to abandon.

A cursory glance at the railway system is sufficient to show that changes are overdue. Certain trains run almost empty year by year, and weekly takings at some stations do not always pay a single day's wages for the staff employed there. Receipts cover only 2 per cent of the cost of the Torrington—Halwill passenger service. If the railways are to play an active part in North Devon's future, they must reorganise radically.

The theory that how the railways are run is a purely domestic matter for themselves is demonstrably invalid. More energetic management in the past might well have led to a more prosperous North Devon today. It would be wrong for this report to be content with stating what railways, and bus replacements, are necessary to the local economy *now*. It is equally important for the area that what remains of the railway system should be viable, worth British Railways' while to keep running well into the future.

STRESS AND STORM

I have just taken my final daylight journey on the branch between Plymouth, Tavistock and Launceston. The rich pattern of memories it evokes took me aback: memories of first boyhood sorties to Dartmoor; of attendances at village functions when I was junior reporter stationed at Plymouth; of journeys for the sake of journeying with mother, sister and fiancée; of adventures into industrial archæology in Bickleigh Vale and Tavistock. The railway seems woven into the very fabric of my life; yet I have known it only during its decline —and but part of that. Its brighter days had already receded deep into history when I took a ticket from Plymouth to Yelverton and had a coach to myself behind a 2—6—2 tank.

I cannot resist retelling its story. As early as 1845, the South Devon Railway (building the broad-gauge line to Plymouth) had prudently proposed a Tavistock branch so as to avert possible narrow-gauge penetration to West Devon. This was only 15 years after the opening of the Liverpool & Manchester Railway, stressing the speed of the Railway Revolution.

In 1848 the broad-gauge interests subscribed to a Plymouth Great Western Dock Company—the docks were, of course, later built—in retaliation to a London & South Western Railway narrow-gauge scheme linking a Plymouth branch *via*

140

Okehampton and Tavistock with a Sutton Harbour development plan. But eventually the fight for Tavistock was between
the South Devon and its former chairman, Thomas Gill. He
had resigned after the rest of the board refused to sanction
further trials of Brunel's unsuccessful atmospheric system,
and now had narrow-gauge backing. Said the press:

'We trust that a timely coalition between the parties will
take place so as to prevent a useless waste of money in the first
instance, and the probable Parliamentary defeat of both in
the next. The ambition of Mr Gill to regain a footing in the
district may be laudable enough, but times, seasons, events
and probabilities should be consulted quite as much as personal whims or lawyers' quarrels.'

Newspaper circulations soared as editors campaigned for
the rival schemes: in 1852 whole pages (eight tightly-packed
columns) were frequently given to reports of meetings.
Friendships were made and broken. Only solicitors thrived.

As foreseen, both schemes were defeated in Parliament in
1853. Gill collected help from far and wide for the next ses-
sion's effort. His scheme was now magnificently entitled the
Plymouth, Tavistock & Devon Central, and would have given
Barnstaple and Bideford direct access to Plymouth. But the
battle was won by the South Devon, with the timely help of
Lord Morley, who struck a personal bargain to aid his own
coffers. (The South Devon built the Lee Moor Tramway for
him—but so poorly that it quickly had to be rebuilt.)

Construction of the single line from Tavistock Junction
near Marsh Mills was slow and costly, engineering works including Shaugh, Yelverton and Grenofen tunnels, and six
large timber viaducts, that at Walkham being 376 yd long
and 132 ft high. Hundreds of workers and horses were employed, but apart from press reports of the occasional brawl,
we can only guess what the invasion of navvies meant to the
villages and hamlets along the route. We do know, however,
that progress was not rapid enough for the mining interests in
Tavistock and the Tamar Valley, and that many people

travelling from Tavistock to Exeter and beyond found it more convenient to catch a coach to Copplestone on the North Devon Railway than to Plymouth.

Opening day was 21 June 1859. The Royal Albert Bridge and the Cornwall Railway had been opened only the previous month, but that did not slacken the appetite for rejoicing. The local newspaper recorded:

'Not a few of the inhabitants of the Plymouth end of the line were willing to make a holiday, and, as the whole people of Tavistock seemed to participate in that feeling, it appears to have been tactfully resolved that all who were on pleasure bent should make that agreeable little town the scene of general festivity. And most assuredly everything was done which could be done to give éclat to an event which will ever-more make the 21st of June one of the brightest red letter days in its annals.'

Regular services started next day. At first the line was busier with minerals than with passengers. Adjoining the Tavistock station was the wealthy Wheal Crelake, whose ores were carried 'at especially favourable rates'. So unimportant was the local passenger traffic that intermediate stations were built only at Bickleigh and Horrabridge. Marsh Mills was added in 1861. Passenger business was, however, boosted by the extension to Launceston in 1865.

Launceston's fortunes had declined deplorably since through traffic had deserted what is now the A30 road, upon the open-ing of the Cornwall Railway. The town worked frantically to be placed on the railway map. Again broad and narrow-gauge interests clashed. After many frustrations, the broad-gauge bill passed the Lords on 30 May 1862. 'We well remember the trial of Queen Caroline . . . and the capture of Sebastopol, but on these occasions there was not the hundredth part felt by Launceston people as at present.'

Victory for the broad gauge was brief. In 1876 the LSWR reached Lydford *via* Okehampton, and had obtained powers to lay a third rail, and run its trains over the broad gauge

G.W.R.

NOTICE.

Passengers joining

Rail Motor Cars

and Trains

at Stations

must obtain

TICKETS

AT THE BOOKING OFFICE.

JAMES MILNE,

Paddington, October, 1931.

General Manager.

500.　　Printed by WYMAN & SONS LTD., London, Reading and Fakenham.—498a.

from there through Tavistock to Plymouth and a handsome new terminus at Devonport.

Such had been the broad gauge's stranglehold on Plymouth, Stonehouse and Devonport that the inhabitants welcomed their second main-line service (albeit routed over the rival's branch) more enthusiastically than the first, though the mere sight of an engine had then been a novelty to many. The Three Towns were *en fête*. All shops and offices closed . . . 'apart from the G.W.R. offices in Fore Street, which, resplendent in front with gilt letters on a black ground, tried to look as if nothing out of the common were going on'.

The track between Lydford and Marsh Mills was still single —as it remains—and station, siding and signalling were hopelessly inadequate. As both gauges' traffic grew, working the railway became ever more complex. For a short time a mineral branch ran from Shaugh Bridge to a quarry at the Dewerstone Rock; and on 11 August 1883 part of the route was further enlivened by the advent of the narrow-gauge Princetown Railway, whose trains at first ran through from the junction to Horrabridge. Throughout the 1880s, the LSWR was fretting for its own independent route to Plymouth. This was opened —*via* Bere Alston—in 1890.

Since then, the original branch between Tavistock and Launceston has had one of the poorest services of any West Country line, the occasional two-coach local puffing up the single track not infrequently being overtaken by aggressive Southerners on their double main line: the two railways run parallel for some miles. But local passenger traffic continued to increase on the Plymouth—Tavistock section until well into the 1930s. When a platform at the junction between the Tavistock and Princetown lines was called Yelverton in 1885, it gave the name to a village which rapidly became an important dormitory for Plymouth. Later halts were added at Plym Bridge, Shaugh Bridge, Clearbrook and Whitchurch: they would of course have been even more useful had they been built in the days of railway supremacy. Services were improved

NARROW GAUGE. *This page from the collection of the author (Part Two) shows Abergynolwyn on the Talyllyn Railway, Stranorlar on the County Donegal Railways, and Douglas on the Isle of Man Railway at the end of business on a stormy summer's evening*

BASSETT - LOWKE. Top: *The engi*
that revolutionised model making, 2 -i
gauge 'Black Prince', produced in 1902.
was later improved and introduced f
other gauges. Middle: *The father of mod*
railways. Bottom: *'Pendennis Castle', bu*
especially for the author (Part One) b
later made a production model

in the 1920s, especially in the early mornings for workers
going to Plymouth, and late in the evening for those returning
from meetings and theatres. An 11.10 p.m. left Millbay for
Tavistock each weekday, while for returning workers a semi-
fast at 5.15 p.m. was at one time followed by a stopping train
all the way to Tavistock only ten minutes later. On Wednes-
days and Saturdays, the regular service of about a train an
hour in each direction was supplemented by specials for
excursionists. Some of these ran through from Plymouth to
Princetown, but most terminated at Yelverton—occasionally
hauled there by a 'Castle'. On fine Bank Holidays and Sundays between the wars, 20,000 Plymouth people would go by
train to destinations between Plym Bridge and Princetown
—and three-quarters of them to Bickleigh, Shaugh Bridge,
Clearbrook and Yelverton.

It is the collapse of this excursion traffic which has robbed
the branch of any place in the Beeching era. Where 20,000
used to go by train, rarely do 200 muster now. This is not
only because people own cars and train services have deterior-
ated: the public's taste in excursions has changed. Once all
guide books to Plymouth waxed warm about Bickleigh Vale,
but probably half of today's Plymothians have never been
there.

The *pièce de résistance* of the journey has always been the
climb through the vale to the Dartmoor foothills. What
scenery the train commands as it climbs and winds through
the rocks and woods, miles from a main road; and what a
hunting-ground for the transport enthusiast, with the railway,
a canal, the route of the pioneer Plymouth & Dartmoor Railway and its Cann Quarry branch, and of the Lee Moor
Tramway, all running together.

For the last time I have followed the familiar curves of
these abandoned transport routes playing hide-and-seek with
one another. The round-faced guard (GWR branch line in
every feature) issued tickets and grimaced at the babies in the
perambulators parked down the gangway of the spacious

147

auto-car, a veritable public hall on wheels—displaying the same GWR notice about passengers joining 'Rail-Motors' at stations having to obtain tickets from the booking office which I first read as a schoolboy. Nothing had changed.

The railway has remained a self-contained little world. It has had its own code of conduct, its own traditions. For many railwaymen (retired and still working) it represents a way of life. During its history of 120 years, including its conception and building, the lives of thousands have been intimately concerned with it, and altered by it. Ghosts will walk—or ride —when it closes on Saturday.

* * *

West Devon's worst blizzard of the century hit the Plymouth to Tavistock and Launceston branch railway on its closing night. This was not a typical railway 'funeral' but a grim and unsuccessful struggle to keep the wheels moving until the end. Over 100 people were stranded when the last trains ever to run on the line failed to reach their destinations.

There could scarcely be a more appropriate finish for the line which has stirred more controversy in its turbulent career of 120 years than any other in the West Country.

The final two scheduled trains did not run at all, and the two previous ones were abandoned—at Tavistock and Bickleigh—after railwaymen had vainly battled for many hours in appalling conditions to keep the tracks clear.

The 6.20 p.m. from Plymouth to Launceston reached Tavistock at 12.25 a.m. yesterday (Sunday) morning, and remains there, the bedraggled 'funeral' wreath still hanging on the front of the locomotive, which may complete the trip today or tomorrow. The 7.10 p.m. from Tavistock to Plymouth was frozen to the ground on Saturday night, but was rescued yesterday afternoon.

Staying in a Dartmoor village, I was cut off by the snow and among those unable to attend. But I followed the dying hours of the branch by telephone. From 8.0 p.m. until 2.30 a.m. I was in constant touch with most of the stations, and gained a broader picture of the line's death throes than I could have done if stuck in one of the trains. As the blizzard howled outside, it was indeed a unique experience to talk to stationmasters long after they should have ceased duty at stations which should by then have been closed for good.

Delays caused by frozen points and poor visibility first became serious about 5.0 p.m., but it was not until 8.0 p.m. that the timetable began to disappear. Surprisingly, the first trouble spot was not on the moorland wilds, but at the junction with the main line at Marsh Mills. The last goods train from Launceston to Plymouth stuck because of point trouble. The 5.40 p.m. passenger train from Launceston was also delayed at Marsh Mills, while the following 7.10 p.m. from Tavistock to Plymouth was kept back at Bickleigh, waiting there to 'cross' the 6.20 p.m. from Plymouth to Launceston.

With 67 passengers in its four coaches, hauled by 2—6—2 tank engine No. 5568, the 6.20 p.m. had left Plymouth an hour late, spent an hour standing still a short distance out of the city, and was again seriously delayed outside Marsh Mills, which it did not reach until 10.35 p.m.—3 h. 10 m. for three miles along the main line, during which time only one train passed on the down road.

It took another hour to struggle up the Vale to Bickleigh, and as already said reached Tavistock at 12.25 a.m. One or two local people had stayed up to see the passing of the era, but the band engaged for the occasion had dispersed long ago.

A signalling failure between Tavistock and Lydford, coupled with the inability of the Lydford stationmaster to reach Tavistock to institute emergency block working (a cutting on the Southern line he was to have used was brimful of snow, and remained blocked for several days), finally ended the chance of the train reaching Launceston. At about 2.0 a.m. the 20 passengers settled down in their compartments for the rest of the night; they were given breakfast by the W.V.S. Those bound for Launceston, including the engine crew, finished the journey in two taxis yesterday afternoon.

As soon as the 6.20 p.m. from Plymouth to Launceston had passed Bickleigh, at about 11.30 p.m., the section was clear for the 7.0 p.m. Tavistock to Plymouth train to continue its journey. But the points were frozen and had to be changed by hand. 'As fast as we dug out the snow, it filled in again,' said Bickleigh's stationmaster, Mr S. Taylor. 'The blizzard was so terrible that we almost collapsed for want of breath.' And when the points were eventually cleared, the engine was unable to move the coaches. Soon after 2.0 a.m., Mr Taylor telephoned to say that the train was to be abandoned. Steam was kept up as long as possible, but as water ran out the engine's fire had to be dropped. The three passengers—all 14-year-old boys—had breakfast in the signalbox. Yesterday afternoon, joined by six other young people who could scarcely believe their luck on seeing a train ready to leave Bickleigh for Plymouth, they were the very last passengers to use the branch. A relief engine and gang had fought their way out from Plymouth in the morning.

These are the bare facts. Behind them, of course, was human drama. People were stranded at all the chief stations —and incidentally sometimes answered the telephone while the staff were out contesting the elements. Passengers were full of praise for the staff; the staff were bitterly disappointed that on this final night, with buses and cars useless, they could not keep the railway going.

In a recent article, I said that ghosts would be abroad on closing night, and so it seemed. At Launceston people waited hours in the snow for the last trains which never came; they recalled that opening day was so wet that the term 'railway weather' is still in the local vocabulary. Up the line, the nocturnal activity reminded one of the 1880s, when the Lydford—Plymouth section was open round the clock to handle the Waterloo—Devonport traffic of the LSWR. Memories of the rivalry between Paddington and Waterloo were renewed in the small hours round signalbox and booking-office fires. Ironically, the Western Region withdraws from

Tavistock and Launceston only a day before the regional boundary adjustments: today the two towns are exclusively in the Southern Region; tomorrow the Western takes control of the entire 'withered arm'.

When tracing the progress of the train up through Bickleigh Vale, I recalled the crowds who once went for picnics at fine weekends; at Yelverton the thousands of convicts who changed *en route* for 'Dartmoor'; at Horrabridge the unemployed miners who joined the trains in the 1880s and 1890s on their way to ply their craft in the New World. And when at length No. 5568 drew into Tavistock's ugly wooden station, I thought of the hopes and fears of Thomas Gill, of the trainloads of ore sent from Wheal Crelake, and of the special which brought 160 troops from Plymouth to quell a miners' rising in 1866.

(*Pictures page 109*)

TIMETABLE THOUGHTS

Basically there are two kinds of service: that operating during most of the day for anyone on any kind of journey over the route; and that provided specifically to carry people on certain particular types of journey. Much of the waste in recent years has been the result of an unhappy compromise between the two.

Where the railway is still popular, it is usually desirable to run a well-balanced service. Passengers expect to find a train at roughly whatever time they wish to travel, and to avoid long gaps it may be necessary to include a few trains which carry only light loads. The number of daily trips required for this kind of service obviously depends on the district: the more prosperous the population and the keener the road competition, the more generous the service which British Railways must run to hold their own. Except in remoter Scotland, five or six well-spaced daily trains are generally the minimum needed to provide adequate choice, and in many more populated areas the minimum is between nine trains and a train each hour.

Relatively few country services now come into this category. Increasingly, country people go by road for miscellaneous journeys, though they may still use trains for particular purposes, such as the daily trip to work, catching long-distance connections, visiting the seaside, or in some districts shopping, usually at well-defined hours.

Clearly there is a point at which the railways should cut their losses and concentrate on serving only what might be termed the 'specialist' traffic. Rarely, however, have officials come to precise decisions. When receipts have dwindled, a service of say ten daily trains has been thinned to eight, and then perhaps to six, though this compares even less favourably with the hourly bus linking the same places. Frequently the individual trains have been removed without any effort at revising the service as a whole.

In 1950, 80 per cent of the passenger traffic on many lines could probably have been retained by a third of the number of trains. Gradually some of the least-used services have been weeded out, but staff still outnumber passengers on many byways at slack times. Even where the public have long abandoned the railway for their general travel, the belief may persist that the timetable should 'look presentable'.

Of course the higher the daily mileage, the lower the cost per mile. But this is not the whole story. The little-used trips which merely 'fill out' the service and keep rolling stock fully employed are expensive if they add to signalling costs; on some lines signalling could be simplified if the freight service were given complete occupation for a couple of hours in mid-morning on Mondays to Fridays. Moreover, running the maximum mileage often hinders correct timing of the most important journeys. One train leaving a market town at 5.40 p.m., soon after the majority of shops and offices close, may well carry more passengers than a 5.20 p.m. and a 6.10 p.m. combined.

Railwaymen sometimes argue that to keep a line open for merely two or three daily trains is uneconomic. Most branches inevitably incur a loss, but if 150 passengers can be attracted to three trains, why augment the loss by carrying only 30 more on double the service? There are indeed lines on which even a single train each way daily, serving commuters and giving a long-distance connection, would make a healthy difference to local life. A diesel locomotive (suitable also for freight work) would be used instead of a multiple unit.

One other point on train services: connections between branches and main lines need to be tightened. Most people are not particularly concerned whether they spend 4 hours or 4 hours 20 minutes in total on a journey, but dislike having to kill the extra 20 minutes at a junction. Slack connections are usually an insurance policy: if one train is late, the passenger stands a better chance of reaching his destination on time. Generally he would prefer British Railways to allow him to take the risk. Many officials do not realise how non-railwaymen value their time. Answering a complaint about poor train-bus connections, the Western Region solemnly published the statement: 'It cannot be said that the present connections are hopeless. Margins of 30 to 40 minutes should not be considered unreasonable.'

BORDER COUNTIES

Visiting Mid-Northumberland in the summer of 1959 for research into the rural transport problem, I was brought into close touch with the Border Counties line, from Hexham to Riccarton Junction. This cross-country byway endeared itself to nearly a century of train lovers, and though I came too late to see it working I found its influence still heavy on the air.

It began as a local concern—great was the aplomb with which the first sod was cut at Tyne Green, Hexham, in 1855—but was completed by the North British Railway as a wedge deep into North Eastern territory. Its construction, especially the last section across the almost uninhabited fells to Riccarton Junction, 800 feet above sea level and two miles from a road, was a battle with geography. This part was opened in 1862 simultaneously with the completion of the Waverley route to Scotland. Eventually the North British obtained running powers into Newcastle, and at one time through trains ran from there to Edinburgh *via* Riccarton and Peebles. But most passengers were on purely local journeys, and even before the first world war the traffic was so thin that several stations became unstaffed halts. The standard service was three trains each way daily, all calling at almost every station —excluding Thorneyburn, for many years a timetable oddity with a single service each way on Tuesdays only. In 41 miles there was only one station where two passenger trains could cross—Reedsmouth, junction for the Wansbeck Valley line to Morpeth.

Reedsmouth station is just within the parish of Birtley, where I worked for a fortnight, and was the first point I visited upon arrival in the district. Driving through the village, I regretted having missed seeing the passenger trains. The Morpeth branch was closed to passengers in 1952, and the Border Counties in 1956. The only trains still running were three goods weekly from Morpeth to Bellingham, reversing at Reedsmouth. The short section between Reedsmouth and Bellingham was thus the sole part of the Border Counties open for any purpose.

I intended to enquire on what days and at what times the goods trains ran, but was pleasantly forestalled. The gate being open, I had driven on to the triangular platform between the two branches, and was trying to evoke the scene at 7.45 on mornings years ago when three trains would stand at the station together. While I was still in the car a whistle sounded from the Bellingham direction. But more, before its echo had died away down the valley, another whistle shrilled, this time from the Morpeth line.

Ghosts of the North British arose during the next few minutes. An inspection train with a handful of officials enjoying a country jaunt pulled in from Bellingham; the thrice-weekly goods came round the curve on the Morpeth line. In addition to the usual single-line crossing manœuvres, both trains had to be reversed. Signal wires squeaked, point rods grunted; steadily the rust of two days was worn off the tracks of the layout—one which must have pleased even the most ambitious North British director. The vast capital tied up in the station, and its imposing signalbox with three tiers of windows, was making one more attempt to seem justified before the inevitable final withdrawal of railways from this outpost of civilisation. To see tracks and points and signals used is satisfying, albeit the movements are not profitable and could be performed in half the time with simpler equipment.

This was the only time I saw the goods; but though virtually trainless, the Border Counties line was still to an extraordinary extent the king-pin of local life. People dated events from its closure, and pointed out how much more cheaply it could run and what hardship the absence of trains had brought to families without cars. Hardship was especially acute at Reedsmouth itself, a railway settlement, most of the houses still owned by British Railways, and well off a bus route. The retired enginemen who had spent their working lives taking others around on their lawful occasions now found themselves unable to reach Bellingham without a long walk or cycle ride or the expense of a taxi. Not only the railway but the community which had grown up round it was in ruins.

I also heard, of course, about the old days, when the railway was respected and big men skilfully coaxed large-wheeled engines up steep gradients, and cleared majestic snowdrifts. I assimilated so much history and legend that eventually each mile of the route assumed individuality; I learnt just who had used every station and why, and what were the idiosyncrasies of the gangers on the bleakest moorland beats and the post-mistresses who held court in offices on station platforms; and wherever I went in the valley of the North Tyne there was the railway intruding itself in the best of the scenery. The grandeur of the engineering works was still apparent—how content the builders must have been with the grace of some of their curves on the bank of the boulder-strewn river!— although decay was far advanced and seemed to set the tone for the whole of the parched, inactive countryside that summer of summers.

The only other train I saw was on my way home at Kielder Forest—just Kielder until 1948 when the 'Forest' was added to publicise the massive forestry project which was transforming the scene for miles around. This was the demolition train, removing the track which several years earlier the Northumberland County Development Plan had asserted would become increasingly busy transporting timber. The plan even discussed whether the single track would be adequate. Meanwhile, instead of three daily trains to the Waverley line at Riccarton Junction, the foresters and their families now had only two buses twice a week. Subsidised by British Railways, these ran to Steele Road, one of the most isolated stations in Britain, but the nearest with road access. A plea to change the destination to Newcastleton, a small market town which could have been reached by an easier road in an additional three minutes at most, was rejected with that perversity so often found in rural transport arrangements. Also, the morning bus was advertised to reach Steele Road a few minutes after the departure of the only train for hours to Carlisle market, although in practice by fast driving a connection was achieved.

BURDEN OF THE PAST

Britain's economy, rural as well as urban, largely developed
round the railway network. With their vast powers of 'creative
destruction', the railways, the first form of mechanical transport, established trends which represented as big a break from

tradition as anything seen in this country. The full significance of the term Railway Age has perhaps not yet been realised.

The first main-line railway was opened in 1830. A mere 30 years later the system of trunk routes was largely completed and its power demonstrated. New towns were rising, and towns bypassed by the trains were declining. Comings and goings between London or provincial capitals and rural areas had intensified at least a dozenfold. Greenwich time had been universally adopted. National newspapers were being increasingly read and greater space was being allotted to national events by local newspapers, aided by the telegraph, a railway adjunct. Many small mills whose future had seemed assured at the beginning of the generation were being forced to close. In short, the processes of centralisation and standardisation had been set in motion.

As the century wore on, even in the remotest countryside, at least in England, people were to some extent affected by the trains. Villages lost trade to towns or to larger villages on the railway map. Carriers working to and from market towns also made station connections: if few passengers were transferred, the occasional intercourse with the outside world was of profound importance, and the exchange of goods increased until railway rates were of concern to farmers everywhere, and manufacturers of popular branded goods could achieve a truly national distribution down to the remotest village shop.

Not only did villages off the railway map turn ever more often to their railhead station, but by 1914 an enormous number of quite small villages and hamlets—in a few cases even individual farms—had their own wayside station or halt. At its peak Britain's railway system was almost absurdly dense, and though few costings were made it is clear that even before the advent of motors much of it never paid. Many rural lines were built by locally-sponsored companies, which eventually sold out to their big neighbours at a price well below the original cost. Others were built by the large concerns themselves, frequently less to serve the local population than to assist manœuvres against rival railways for the profitable long-distance traffic. Thus some of the branch lines in Mid-Northumberland were originally envisaged as through routes to Scotland. The duplication of routes between towns was often economically unjustified, but each new line did carry trains into a further slice of countryside.

For two generations the railways held an almost complete monopoly. They wielded unparalleled power which they frequently abused. Although there were highlights, especially on the technical side, generally services were improved only when imperative, and there was little voluntary exertion to satisfy the public. Mechanical transport developed as one of the least efficient and most quarrelsome of industries. But from the beginning many railwaymen acknowledged that monopoly involved responsibilities as well as privileges, and though opportunities to help both themselves and their customers were ignored, the tradition of providing some services which would inevitably lose money was established. The railways themselves, of course, were sole judge of what charity should be meted out to a minority of travellers at the cost of the customers at large. From this tradition have stemmed many of the industry's difficulties in the last forty years.

If before 1910 the railways could prosper while being inefficient, tightfisted with most of their customers, and extravagant in rivalry with their neighbours, they could not do so once motor vehicles had proved themselves. But management was slow to realise the seriousness of the challenge—quite unprepared for the invasion of the roads by motor buses after 1918. On some routes the railways lost the cream of local traffic by 1925, but little was done either to fight back or to reduce the size of the system. Pruning was hardly started before 1930, and even then caution prevailed.

Undoubtedly, had the management of the four big railway companies of the 1923-47 Grouping Era been able to cast aside past traditions, practices and prejudices, rural dead

161

wood would have been cut far more firmly, to conserve resources for the competition with road transport on the main fronts. But officials still thought, as some do even now, in terms of monopoly, involving certain duties as well as privileges. To run a railway as any other business, ignoring the broader public benefit, was a notion few entertained. Other factors of course limited the effectiveness of railway competition between the wars, but management voluntarily continued to accept the obligation of supplying unremunerative services in thinly-populated areas.

The war and nationalisation brought little change in outlook. When the Transport Commission were formed, they were charged with providing 'adequate railway services' throughout the country, the needs of agriculture and the rural population being borne in mind. In 1953, however, the requirement of adequacy was dropped. The Commission were then technically free to run what railway services they chose, subject to the Transport Users' Consultative Committee procedure, and to the two general statutory duties of securing enough revenue to 'make provision for the meeting of charges properly chargeable to revenue, taking one year with another' and having 'due regard . . . to the needs of the public, agriculture, commerce and industry'. As the Select Committee on Nationalised Industries pointed out in 1960, these two duties conflicted. 'In having regard to the public need, the Commission are providing services which detract from their chances of making their revenue match their expenditure'.

Until the end of 1961 the Commission themselves continued to assess the 'public need'. Little fresh blood had been drafted to the top levels of railway management; most district superintendents, for example, had joined the service when it was still conceived in terms of monopoly. Moreover, a high proportion of the executive staff were still in the territory where they had begun their careers. It is therefore not surprising that social obligations should have been regarded seriously, many services covering less than a third of their

PADDINGTON TO SEAGOOD—I. *The buffer stops at the two termini of the Paddington to Seagood model railway*

PADDINGTON TO SEAGOOD—II. Top: *Another view of Padding-ton*. Middle: *'Blackbird' at the 'country station'*. Bottom: *'The Company' at Seagood*

costs being allowed to survive.

There was another factor. Throughout the 1950s a strong belief persisted among railwaymen at all levels that in the end the Government would recognise the desirability of maintaining the system substantially as it was and grant some kind of general subsidy. That the question of 'social transport' obligations was shunned so long—avoided even in the 1960 White Paper—was a hard blow to officials trying to keep their industry intact. Uncertainty discouraged economies, for most economy schemes involve capital expenditure only justifiable where services are to continue at least for a few years. Yet certainly many worthwhile savings, and adaptations of services to meet changed conditions, could have been made even on a short-term basis. When the staff of the Lake District Transport Enquiry studied the railways of that area in 1960, the impression was gained of an organisation lacking in enthusiasm to make the best of the situation. A large proportion of the staff with whom we talked were chiefly concerned to point out missed opportunities.

With the appointment of Dr Richard Beeching as chairman of the Transport Commission in 1961, a new era began, the railways setting out to run on strictly commercial lines for the first time in their history. A vast programme of research was inaugurated, the railways themselves undertaking fact-finding of a kind which in this country had previously been attempted only by the author. The Minister of Transport, not the Transport Commission, became the judge of social requirements.

During the 1950s many people had thought in terms of a general subsidy to British Railways to cover all social, strategic and other uneconomic requirements. But the writing of a blank cheque had everything against it. A subsidy would almost inevitably be too small to plug mounting losses, or so large that prodigious sums of the taxpayers' money would vanish without adequate control over its results.

It was the author who first suggested that while British

Railways as a whole should be expected to run strictly as a business concern, subsidy should be distributed 'in a number of grants for limited, specified purposes, enabling the railways to retain, modernise, and in a few cases perhaps even reopen, branch lines and wayside stations which have a value to the public'. At first this idea of specific subsidies for specific lines met little approval, partly because at that time many people still felt that the railways themselves should remain the assessor of public need, and partly because of the difficulty of producing accurate accounts for one line. Railway accountancy has advanced since then, and the latter difficulty is now largely removed.

*   *   *

Since the war more people have offered advice on how to run branch lines than on any other subject of comparable commercial importance. Railway enthusiasts, passengers, would-be passengers, and even motorists who never use trains seem to think they have the key to the railways' rejuvenation and have produced a welter of contradictory suggestions.

Most of the clamour has arisen out of self-interest, and most has had to be ignored; but with a few outstanding exceptions, the impression has been given that not even the saner suggestions from responsible organisations and individuals have been taken seriously. Not only have the public's views been largely brushed aside, but until 1962 British Railways undertook practically no fact-finding themselves to establish the true position of rural services.

It would be possible to formulate broad principles for the efficient running of a branch line as for any other business, but little more is understood of the subject now than was known in the 1850s and 1860s. Incredibly, in 1959 I was the first person to discover how the closing of a branch affected the travel habits of its former users. Despite repeated arguments about the amount of inconvenience caused, neither British Railways nor the opponents of their closure policy had seen fit to find the facts even in a specimen case.

An impressive point is that while expert advice is readily available to any farmer, and is often offered even when not positively requested, for decades no senior officials—nobody paid a salary comparable to that of Agricultural Advisory Service officers—has shown more than the most cursory interest in the wellbeing of many country stations. (Taking an annual trip in a non-stopping inspection saloon whose timetable is known in advance does not, of course, reveal very much.) While productivity has leapt forward on the farms, work goes on at the stations much as it did in Victorian times. The comparison might be taken a step further. The N.A.A.S. employs specialist economists and the study of specimen accounts has become a fine art, while the work of the officers in the countryside is backed by projects at universities and research establishments. The transport equivalents have been almost wholly confined to the engineering side; no work at all had been done before 1960 on the economics of railway working in rural areas, except where specific possible closures were being investigated. The Ministry of Transport had no expert advice on which to call; it undertook no fact-finding itself.

Had a commercial firm known as little about a substantial part of its activities as British Railways knew about their secondary and branch lines until 1962, bankruptcy would have been inevitable. The malaise has stemmed from various roots: Government policy was uncertain, the railways lacked leaders with enthusiasm and foresight, and though large sums of capital have been poured into the industry, money has been short for urgent schemes.

It is easy to curse the politicians, but the Government line might have been different—or at least more decisive—had top railwaymen really demanded action. The trouble probably goes back to poor selection of staff between the wars. It is no accident that many of the more efficient officers in high positions during the 1950s began their careers with the North Eastern Railway, the only pre-1923 company fully to realise the value of fresh blood.

While industry has increasingly appointed specialists and encouraged graduates by allowing them to start several rungs up the ladder, until recently nearly all railwaymen were recruited at the lowest school-leaving level. Jobs which industry would automatically allot to specially-trained experts have often gone to railwaymen in general offices with no qualifications. Ability has seldom been amply rewarded, length of service—coupled it is said with physical stature!—being the key to promotion. Lack of talent at the top and frustration among men lower down has led to many of the best staff leaving for other jobs.

It is thus that we find chief district officials bogged down with the real and imaginary difficulties which surround them. This is why stock reasons against making changes are trotted out before a proposal is properly considered—why a proposal has to be rejected lest the public should construe it as a precedent.

Failure to be alert and interested has often led to poor relations between staff at district headquarters and those outside. In many areas the gulf is absolute. Stationmasters have long ceased passing even minor suggestions to headquarters, which in return do not bother to consult them on timetable changes.

Experience has not always been pooled even between adjacent districts, let alone between Regions. The Regions have gone their separate ways. Thus the London Midland either keep a station fully staffed or close it completely, refusing to introduce the unstaffed halts common elsewhere, while at one time the Western Region spent up to five times as much as the Eastern Region on annual maintenance of branches closed to passengers and used only by light freight traffic. Regional jealousies have often prevented the cheapest and smoothest working of traffic in border areas, and regional 'pride' has been costly in other ways. For example, when the Southern took over the Western lines in the Weymouth area, they immediately changed the quite modern Western signals for

Southern ones—although most of the engine drivers over the route continued to be Western men.

But perhaps the worst waste of all has arisen from lack of co-ordination between engineering and commercial departments covering the same territory. During the 1950s several branch lines were extensively relaid or resignalled shortly before closure. At one station—Clifton Mill on the London Midland Region—the office was actually being enlarged to take a new stove which had just arrived, two days before total closure. Many slightly less extreme examples could be quoted —though probably not in the North Eastern and Scottish Regions.

* * *

There is virtually no administrative system for most branches. Individual officers at district headquarters consult (or do not consult) individual station-masters along the route. Nearly all of the dozens of station-masters I have interviewed during survey work have criticized the lack of contact between themselves and district offices. It should be added that many station-masters are merely dignified porters—occasionally the station-master is now the sole employee—and not necessarily men one might readily expect to exercise authority and judgment.

The most useful single move would be steadily to abolish individual station-masters and to appoint a linemaster responsible for the day-to-day administration of an entire line or run of intermediate stations on the main line. The advantages would be numerous. While station-masters at adjoining stations may regard each other as rivals, a linemaster would see his line as an entity and would be consulted by district headquarters on matters concerning it. Total staff costs would be reduced, only porters being employed at most stations; but the linemaster would rank higher than individual station-masters, and a higher grade of man could be retained on the job than is now possible in the countryside. He would be given a car for visiting his various stations, would also regularly visit district headquarters, and would attend conferences with other linemasters. (Already some station-masters control a number of small stations, but this proposal introduces a new principle.)

A linemaster, sometimes speaking directly to the district superintendent, would be able forcibly to call attention to weak points in the timetable, and to resist changes which would upset regular travellers. He would know just who these travellers were, and might be able better than other railway-men to suggest a compromise to satisfy them and meet the requirements of district headquarters for a new junction connection time, for example. The best London connection would be less likely to be missed narrowly, year by year; stations would be more likely to display train departure times. Excursion facilities could be brought closer to the demand. The advice of a linemaster might prevent unnecessary expenditure on renewals and repairs.

More stations could be reduced to unstaffed halts, tickets being issued on the trains. (A little adaptability could overcome possible hitches: for instance, the linemaster might travel on the first up train on Monday mornings to help issue the weekly season tickets.) Station buildings need simplifying: in some cases to erect a small new building would be cheaper than to keep up the existing range. Cheap fare facilities need rationalization: printing and other costs could often be cut if a single fare were quoted from a group of stations instead of individual fares varying by an odd copper or two. In some cases country stations might stock the junction's excursion tickets, of course also issuing passengers with a ticket to the junction: 'rebooking' at junctions to take advantage of their better range of cheap tickets artificially reduces the receipts of some branches.

RAILWAY PUBLISHING

Railway enthusiasts take their literature seriously, and because so many of them are experts on some aspect themselves, they are apt to be severely critical. On balance this is good. It is right that authors and publishers should be kept on their toes to see that the information dispensed in books is accurate, that parts of the subject have not been omitted or glossed over too lightly—even that the choice of pictures is representative.

Yet there is a danger that in making certain we have all the right ingredients in the right proportions we fail to pay the necessary attention to the final baking. Though accuracy is important, so are readability and a sense of perspective. Dare

I say it, there is little to choose between a dull book with all its facts in orderly correctness, and a well-written one which thoroughly brings its subject to life yet is not 100 per cent reliable in detail. If a publisher might be allowed one plea, it is that reviewers and readers should judge a work as a whole. Reviewers who give prominence to minor mistakes without assessing the success or failure of a book according to the author's own objectives—of course a different writer would have produced a different work—do not give the constructive guidance that might help raise future standards.

Every reader is a potential critic; every reader has his own ideas about what the length should be, what themes should be developed, and how many photographs should be included.

Text continued on p. 1

Impression by Mr C. Hamilton Ellis of a passenger train on the North Wales Narrow Gauge Railways headed by the 0—6—4 tank locomotive *Moel Tryfan,* from *The Welsh Highland Railway,* by Charles E. Lee.

The pictures on pages 172 to 177 are from books published by David & Charles, of which the author is a director

WORK IN PROGRESS ON THE TALYLLYN RAILWAY, 1952
(From *Railway Adventure*, by L. T. C. Rolt). Top: *Re-laying the loop
at Abergynolwyn station.* Bottom: *'Total Occupation': Rebuilding the
bridge at Brynglas station*

AROUND STRABANE (From *The County Donegal Railways,* by E. M. Patterson). Top: *Railcar No. 14 and trailers Nos. 6 and 3, on train from Stranorlar crossing Mourne River bridge, August 1952.* Bottom: *No. 3, 'Lydia', entering Strabane from Londonderry, August 1952*

HIGHLAND MISCELLANY (From *The Highland Railway*, by H. A. Vallance). Top: *Inverness, after arrival of night train from London in 1906.* Middle: *Board marking Druimuachdar Summit.* Bottom: *Badengorm Burn accident on 18 June 1914*

FOREST OF DEAN GOODS TRAINS (From *The Severn & Wye Railway*, by H. W. Paar). Top: *West-bound train at Drybrook Road, 1922*. Middle: *Beginning the long climb from Coleford Junction with the branch goods, 1948*. Bottom: *North-bound p.w. train at Parkend*

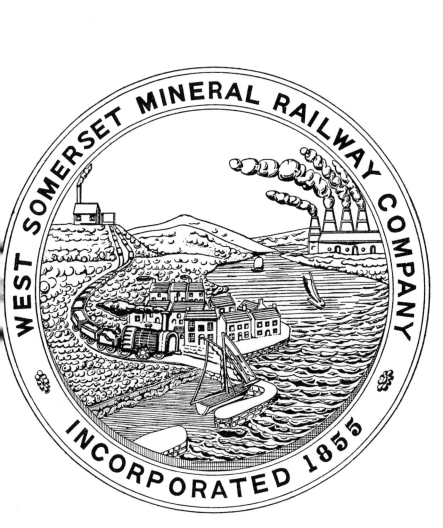

Company seal from *The West Somerset Mineral Railway*
by Roger Sellick

The customer's views are interesting and often extremely helpful; but I wonder if it is always appreciated what consultations go on behind the scenes before it is decided to present the history of a railway, for example, in its published form.

The mere question of length often requires careful consideration. It is axiomatic that the author who has spent years collecting information on a minor line and is anxious to pack in almost every single fact may not produce the most worthwhile book. Selection is half the art of history. Another vital point is that history is only worth the use that is made of it. To my mind a highly detailed book which is beyond the palate and pocket of all but the keenest enthusiasts may be less useful than a more general study which is bought and read by local as well as railway historians. One of the big difficulties in writing and publishing on railways is to cater simultaneously for the expert and the general reader. It helps to gather the more technical information into self-contained paragraphs and appendices easily skipped if desired; maintaining a happy balance deserves more care than it is often given.

Some subjects provide scope for both popular and more erudite works; others will clearly support only one volume in the foreseeable future, and it would be mischievous to cream off the interest with a short account lacking important details. When we have to compromise, it is my belief that we should occasionally err on the side of pleasing the reader who is not an enthusiast but realises that local history does not make sense without railways. Indeed, I think railway authors and publishers have a unique opportunity to fill in a corner of Britain's social and economic history and to inspire others to follow suit on different subjects. For example, even in the sphere of transport history, the study of roads is still neglected.

HIGHLAND LUXURY

Holidays which involve Euston have a habit of starting on a depressing note. We had to pick our way through a sea of trolleys and loitering porters to the sleeping car. The attendant was absent, his urn spouting boiling water on to the floor; it was a pre-war car with rattling partitions and a choice between hot air and hot air. The train started on time, but spent ten minutes on the first mile or so, and being an hour and a half late before Rugby we dozed off assuming that already we had lost our 70-minute connection at Perth.

Scotland quickly made amends. We caught our connection, with a six instead of a 70-minute wait; a fair exchange. We were away on the Highland line to Inverness, a compartment to ourselves, no daily paper, but a current timetable and a copy of the 1894 edition of Murray's *Handbook for Travellers in Scotland*—and a pair of rail-rover tickets. Our plans went no further; we were playing it off the cuff.

The first decision was to alight at Ballinluig to 'do' the Aberfeldy branch. We were the only passengers on the single coach hauled by a two-year-old express-size diesel locomotive; the guard stood by our side in the corridor relating local history and pointing to the Tay's most famous fishing reaches. At Aberfeldy the stationmaster volunteered to keep back the return train for five minutes to give us a chance to see the village; at a pinch we could have longer, he said, but that would rob the guard of his lunch break. It turned out that the guard lived within a stone's throw of Grandtully, one of the intermediate stations, where a 12-minute wait was scheduled, ostensibly for shunting purposes. 'They keep the stop, though it isn't often we have anything to shunt,' said the driver, using the break to take us over his machine, spotless in hydro-electric station style.

Back at Ballinluig, we sat in the porters' room beside a blazing coal fire, welcome enough that chilly August. 'You couldn't have done what you've just done last year,' a ganger eating sandwiches told us. Extra trains had been provided for 'the holiday crowds' in the 1962 summer service. We had found them useful, certainly; indeed, I shall always remember that trip up the track on the banks of the wandering Tay. But where were the holiday crowds?

The diesel was prepared for another trip to Aberfeldy: eventually it left without a single passenger. A lightly-loaded express raced through the station on its way from Glasgow to Inverness only 45 minutes behind the Edinburgh—Inverness train which we had used from Perth to Ballinluig. And half an hour later, we were aboard a third restaurant-car train for Inverness. The total complement of passengers including ourselves was nine. At 1.0 p.m. we sat down in an otherwise empty restaurant car.

We were greeted royally by the crew, who gave us an imaginative meal exhibiting real preparation and cooking—at á-la-càrte prices coming to less than we should have paid for a mass-produced affair on a table d'hôte car. We complimented the conductor on the fresh-fruit salad. 'Don't carry a can-opener on the car,' he said. 'I tell the chef to get cutting. He's nothing else to do anyway.'

This was railway Scotland at its best. But joy was spoilt by the knowledge that such luxurious personal service for a few individualists like ourselves could not continue much longer. Indeed, when we worked out what our morning's transport and lunch must have cost British Railways, we felt we were guilty of protracting the expensive death throes of an anachronism. Should we not have conformed and used that 40-seater coach whose driver was giving a running commentary on the scenery into a microphone while threading his tortuous way along the parallel road?

Our own guide, as always on railway holidays, was old John Murray. He temporarily put Dr Beeching's plans to rationalise British Railways into the background. Could we see the Pass of Killiecrankie from our table? Said the *Handbook*: 'At the N. end, the rly. is conveyed over a small burn on a noble *Viaduct* of 10 arches, bending l. before a tunnel is entered, and from this viaduct the whole Pass can be seen by looking back.' We read on in anticipation. 'Leaving Struan, the rly. begins to ascend, more slowly at first, rapidly afterwards, more than 800 ft. being ascended in 12 m. The first 2 m. are through a birch plantation—*Clunes* rt.; then the country becomes much wilder and more desolate, and trees are not seen again until Glen Truim and Strathspey. . . . The Garry is crossed; snow posts and strong palisade screens for the rly. against snow-drifts testify to the severity of the winter in these parts, and well-marked moraines are seen. . . . At 53 m. "the summit, 1484 ft." is passed and the train hastens down the Pass of Drumouchter, "by far the wildest scene through which any rly. passes in this country" (*Geikie*). . . .'

Murray had the skill not only to tell you what you wanted to know, but to give you pride in personally having traversed the trail with him. It goes without saying, of course, that modern guides do not cater in such detail for the railway traveller. The fact that most of Murray's *Routes* are railway routes is one reason why I set high value on his *Handbooks*. Another is that they are written more interestingly and objectively, and are far more thorough, especially on subjects other than conventional tourist attractions, than recent counterparts.

It was easier to be objective—to write about Scotland almost as if it were a far foreign country—in the late nineteenth century. For one thing Victorians took their travel seriously; for another, tourists did not spill all over the countryside but kept mainly to well-defined tracks and resorts specially created for them. 'At all the important points good hotels, sometimes rising to the magnitude of palaces, have been erected, while, where possible, railways and steamers convey travellers into the very heart of the mountains,' writes Murray. But always the traveller was segregated from local life. Save for the employment they provided, the giant tourist expresses which struggled over the Highland line, often hours late, the luxuriously-appointed pleasure steamers on the lochs, and the grand hotels which may one day be recognised as a valuable part of Scotland's architectural heritage, had little more influence on the community than the aeroplanes which fly overhead today.

Undoubtedly it was all highly artificial; but it was also colourful. Mr H. A. Vallance captures something of the atmosphere of those hectic pioneer days of mass Highland travel in his *The Highland Railway* (see the period-piece illustration at the top of page 175), but the full story remains to be told, and will probably not be set down until it recedes further into history and the superbly-engineered tracks through the wilds of some of Britain's finest scenery are given back to nature.

INVERNESS.

The Highland Railway Company's
STATION HOTEL.

Patronised by their Royal Highnesses the Prince and Princess of Wales,
the Duke of Cambridge Prince and Princess Christian,
and other Members of the Royal Family, and by most of the Nobility of Europe.

This Large and Handsome Hotel, adjoining the Station, with all the modern Improvements, and elegantly Furnished, is acknowledged to be one of the best appointed in the Kingdom. Has recently undergone extensive Additions and Alterations, and contains numerous Suites of comfortable and lofty Apartments. A new elegant Coffee-room, Drawing-room Smoking and Billiard-rooms, Lavatories, and Bath rooms.

Pianos are at the free disposal of the occupants in every Private Sitting-room.

Parties leaving in the morning can go over the grand Scenery along the Skye Railway, or visit either Loch-Maree, Gairloch, Dunrobin, or Golspie, and return the same day to the Hotel.

Table d'Hôte at 6.30 and 7.30; on Sundays at 5 p.m. only.

AN OMNIBUS ATTENDS THE STEAMERS.
HOTEL PORTERS ATTEND AT THE STATION.
POSTING

TARIFF:

SITTING-ROOMS—Ground Floor, per Day 5s	LUNCHEONS and SUPPERS—Cold Meat 1s 6d
Do. —1st Floor . 7s 6d to 10s	Soup . . . . . . 1s and 1s 6d
BEDROOMS—1st „ . . 3s 6d	DINNERS—From the Joints . 2s 6d
Do. —2nd „ . . 3s 0d	Soups, Fish, Entrées, &c., &c., as per daily bill
Do. —3rd „ . . 2s 6d	of fare, at proportionally moderate charges.
If two Persons occupy one Bed, 1s extra.	TABLE D'HÔTE 4s 6d
BOARD—Plain BREAKFASTS & TEAS. 1s 6d	SPECIAL DINNERS in Private Sitting-
Do., with Cold Meat or Broiled	Rooms from 5s
Ham 2s	
Do., with Chops or White Fish, 2s 6d	A large assortment of choice WINES as per
Do., with Salmon, Steak, or	List.
Ham and Eggs, or Chicken	FIRES—Sitting-room, 1s 6d; Bedroom, 1s.
with Ham and Tongue 3s	BATHS—Hot, 1s 6d; Cold, 1s; Hip or
TABLE D'HÔTE Breakfast . . 3s	Sponge, 6d.

SERVICE—A charge of 1s 6d per day will be made to Visitors occupying Rooms. In other cases, 3d per Meal.

A Large Comfortable Room is provided for Commercial Gentlemen.

EDWARD CESARI, Manager.

In the fullness of time, to be precise in 4 hours 26 minutes, we completed the 120 miles from Ballinluig *via* Forres to Inverness. One other passenger was left to alight with us. At station after station we had stopped without transacting business—and the Wick line's train on the opposite platform reminded me that the previous year we had travelled to the farther north and back in trains never used by more than a dozen people at a time, with restaurant cars where again we had been the sole diners. But the busy Inverness enquiry office showed that while few may tour Scotland by rail for the sheer pleasure of the journeys, the demand for sleepers and car sleepers still embarrassingly outstrips the supply at peak periods. And so to the Station Hotel, one of the few services started by the Highland Railway which has fully adapted itself to today's requirements.

(Pictures page 175)

WEST COUNTRY NOTEBOOK

(A random selection from the author's
newspaper work)

A friend has sent me a picture (page 109) of an excursion train crossing a wooden viaduct near Hayle just a hundred years ago. Investigations show that it was the first excursion to run on the newly-opened West Cornwall Railway. It carried the combined Redruth and Camborne temperance societies for a day's outing to Hayle Towans, and a local inhabitant composed a special song for the remarkable occasion. After noting that the rails were laid 'fit to carry an English Queen and fit to carry the Poor', it continued:

> Steam is up and we are ready;
> See, the engine puffing goes !
> Keep your heads cool, and be steady;
> Mind your caps and mind your clothes.

Apparently there were about 20 verses—a bagatelle compared with the train's 76 vehicles!—but the full work has been denied to posterity. The chorus, however, is still sometimes remembered by old Camborne people:

> Happy Camborne, happy Camborne,
> Where the railway is so near;
> And the engine shows how water
> Can accomplish more than beer.

Three engines were provided for the monster procession. Only a few of the 76 vehicles were orthodox coaches, the rest being open trucks with planks. One parson was reputed to be so large that he occupied the whole plank at the end of a truck. On the return journey, the three engines found their task too much, and the cavalcade ground to a halt beside an orchard. In the words of a contemporary commentator: 'It may have been their extreme anxiety to take measures against such an intoxicating beverage as cider, but at all events that army of teetotallers swarmed down from the trucks and up the apple trees until the orchard resembled the famous cupboard of Mother Hubbard.' (1952)

*   *   *

Receipts at a station on a Devon branch line seldom cover the wages of a porter-signalman, let alone contribute to the cost of running trains and maintaining track; but it would be wrong to think that the porter must find time heavy on his hands. His tasks are numerous.

It so happens that the station is situated near a public house, an amenity not enjoyed by the staff further up the line. Several times a day the porter answers the telephone to receive messages such as 'I'm turrable thirsty, Bill. Send 'long a couple o' ziders.' The bottles go on one train and return as empties with the cash on the next. Newspapers and groceries are also bought and despatched for those working at more lonely spots. A churn of water has to be placed on the first train of the day for a crossing-keeper's house with no supply.

Then, as a keen amateur horticulturist, the porter not only tends his own plot at the bottom of the embankment but also has to answer the telephone queries from other railwaymen tilling the ground between trains. Spare plants and seeds, and sometimes even kittens or ferrets, are exchanged with the ready co-operation of the guard, who accepts that the railway is the 'common carrier'. (1952)

*   *   *

A lady visited a South Devon railway station to enquire the

time of the 'next' through train to Newcastle. She wasn't in a hurry, she said, but it must be a through train.

'No through trains, my dear,' said the booking clerk. 'You'll have to change at Bristol.'

'But there must be a through train,' persisted the lady.

'Well, there'll be one on Saturdays in the summer. In July, I expect,' came the reply.

'That'll do fine,' said the lady, and went her way. (1953)

* * *

People are ready enough to blame the railways when delays occur because traffic is too heavy, but probably most Cornish growers are too concerned at their own loss to think about that made by the Transport Commission as the result of the failure of the broccoli crop. At this time of year there should be a steady stream of express freights—railwaymen call them 'broc specials'—running from West Cornwall to London and the Midlands. In anticipation of the rush, engines, men and rolling stock were deployed at various points in the Plymouth District, and because of the frost most of them are now superfluous. The loss runs into many thousands of pounds. (1956)

* * *

When British Railways seek to close a branch line these days, they exhibit an announcement couched in formally unpalatable language with the alluring heading 'Public Notice'. How different was the tone displayed by the GWR in 1928. I quote in full an announcement of that year.

'The Great Western Railway Company give Notice that they have in contemplation the closing of the Yealmpton branch between Plymstock and Yealmpton. The reason for this is that the revenue from the traffic on the branch does not meet the working expenses and the business is showing a definite downward trend. The company appreciate that the closing of the branch will involve withdrawal of a facility which is of value to the public and traders of the district, and they are prepared therefore to receive suggestions for increasing the passenger, parcels, and merchandise traffic. To this end they will defer coming to a definite decision to close the line until January 1 next, but if the loss continues this will be inevitable. Meanwhile, should there be a desire to discuss the matter with the company's officers, a public meeting will be arranged, but if the various interests in the district wish the line to be kept open it should be recognised that it must be used more than has been the case during the last two years.'

*　　　*　　　*

Because of engineering work, for some weeks the *Cornishman* from the Midlands to Penzance and Kingswear has been diverted to an alternative route between Birmingham and Cheltenham, and this sometimes causes delay. British Railways have therefore officially retimed the express on the rest of its route to the West. In fact it often happens, as it did on Saturday, that it gains time between stations. I joined the Kingswear portion at Exeter. Of the 25 minutes it spent in the station, 15 would have been unnecessary had it been allowed to leave at the time shown in the timetable rather than that in the supplement. The guard complained that the better the performance of the engine, the longer they had to hang around at stations waiting for the retarded departure time, which most passengers naturally regarded as late. The official view is that as the express may be 20 minutes behind the timetable schedule some days, it should be standardised so always. But at that reckoning every train should always be held back to take as long as it does in high summer congestion or winter fog and snow. (1957)

*　　　*　　　*

Railway engines are built to last. The Western's 'Kings' celebrated their 30th birthday last year when they were still exclusively in charge of expresses such as the *Cornish Riviera*. Now comes the diamond jubilee of the introduction of another class famous in the West Country. The 'T9s', often known as the 'Greyhounds', are not only the oldest express class still at work on British Railways today, but also one of the most beautiful. There were 66 of them altogether, all built by 1901, and it speaks volumes for their designer, Dugald Drummond, that every one survived to be included in British Railways' stock at nationalisation. Occasionally they still haul light express trains, but most of those still in service are on branch-line duties, especially on the Southern system between Exeter, Okehampton and Padstow, where remarkably high speeds are often achieved on short sections between stations. (1958)

*　　　　*　　　　*

With feet covered with white clay and hair reeking of smoke and sulphur fumes, a group of railway enthusiasts arrived at St Blazey considerably behind schedule on Saturday evening after a tour of some of the railways which serve the Cornish china-clay industry. There were, however, no complaints, the white dirt collected at one end of the body and the black dirt at the other end being accounted part of the day's enjoyment, and the lateness of the special train demonstrating vividly the difficulties which British Railways face in carrying the china-clay traffic.

The excursion was so popular that the organisers, Plymouth Railway Circle, had to refuse bookings, 93 people being considered the maximum which could be carried with even passable comfort in the string of goods guards' vans which composed the train. The trip began at Fowey, a pannier-tank locomotive making a noisy exit from Arthur Quiller-Couch's Troy Town station and battling its way up the steep incline to Pinnock Tunnel, the *pièce de résistance* of the itinerary. 1,173 yards long, steeply graded and with almost continuous curves, the tunnel is reputed to be the nearest to hell you can get in Cornwall, but though the passengers were soon spluttering from the sulphurous fumes, they were reluctant to take shelter in the closed section of the guards' vans. 'A wonderful experience', was the general verdict upon emerging into fresh air again. Normally the line is used only by clay trains: about eight full and eight empties a day.

After waiting for a china-clay train running late at St

Blazey, the special joined the Par-Newquay line for the climb up Luxulyan Bank, passing under the graceful arches of the 120-year-old Treffry Viaduct, built for posterity and intact though disused, and then followed the goods-only Carbean branch wandering erratically across the moor between the clay pits and tips. Railway working, it is said, is never uninteresting, but its enjoyment requires patience, as during the shunting before the final descent to Carbean. The engine had to change ends of the train, and leave three vehicles behind lest it should fail to summon power enough for the return trip, on a layout patently designed to tax the ingenuity of shunters and guards, much of the manoeuvring having to be accomplished by gravity. And so it was again at Carbean. Some of the keenest enthusiasts might cheerfully have camped on the train had the hitching and unhitching continued all night; others with appointments back in civilisation decided that being an hour late already they must wend their own ways back to St Austell. (1961)

*   *   *

Fireworks, fog signals, diesel horns, bugles, top hats, 'Auld Lang Syne', wreaths, mock sandwich-board men proclaiming 'The End is at Hand', cameras, tape recorders, and a lurid representation of 'Dr Beeching's axe'—these all contributed to Saturday's festive funeral of the Helston branch. Railway enthusiasts, who had travelled from far and wide to see that the last trains were accorded full honours, acclaimed it 'the best burial to date' in the West Country.

The proceedings began with crowds assembling for the departure of the 8.45 p.m. from Helston. Money piled high in the booking office as people bought tickets for souvenirs as well as for the final trip to Gwinear Road and back. One man alone acquired 56 assorted low-priced tickets, many of them printed in GWR days. A local woman bought one to send to her sister now living in Canada; many potted biographies were given through the ticket hatch.

Hats were raised as the 'funeral procession' formally paced

down the platform. The full-dress mourners were former boys of Helston Grammar School who had once used the train daily. 'We represent all stations on the branch', they said, proffering the wreath for inspection: 'In loving memory of the Helston-Gwinear Road express'. Doors closed, the signal turned to green, and amid the explosion of fireworks and detonators the six-coach 8.45 p.m. moved on its noisy way. . . .

While waiting for main-line connections at Gwinear Road, groups of the 300 passengers sang 'For Auld Lang Syne' on the platform. Four people transferred from the 2.30 p.m. from Paddington: three genuine travellers who would have had the branch train to themselves had it not been closure night, and the clerk of a parish council who jokingly displayed a large 'For Sale' notice. Then it was 'Auld Lang Syne' at all stations and halts back to Helston—and sharp whistles from the guard who disliked passengers leaving their compartments.

'I'll be glad when tonight is over,' he said. He himself will remain one of the evening's memories. No inspector or even stationmaster being on duty, he bore the full brunt of the passengers' criticisms of a 'typical British Railways muddle'. Normally the last train spent the night at Helston, but the enthusiasts thought that after the closure it would work back to Gwinear Road, and they asked permission to travel by it —as they had done in similar cases at other branch-line funerals. Plymouth office, however, was adamant that the train would not be returning. In fact it did return. But passengers were prevented from using it. 'It's advertised as an empty train, and if you get on it, it won't be empty,' carefully explained the harassed guard.

After a final burst of song at Helston, diesel D6312—displaying the wreath—duly set off into the night with its empty coaches. The station staff turned off the lights and went home. But that was not quite the end. The privately-run refreshment room had been granted an extension licence to commemorate its closure. Tongues wagged on about British Railways and

Dr Beeching. And outside in the station yard, buses and cars were entangled in a chaotic jam. It was here, of course, that the first railway-sponsored bus service began, in 1903. A plaque records the innovation which was the railways' own undoing. (1962)

*   *   *

My picture (middle right of page 110) shows a train on the most westerly railway in England about 60 years ago. The German-built engine is returning empty from Newlyn Harbour near Penzance to collect another load from Penlee stone quarry. At that time the engine was unnamed, but at the outbreak of the first world war she was christened *Penlee* to disguise her German origins. Upon retirement about 30 years ago she was exhibited on a concrete pedestal at the quarry entrance, and there she still stands, though souvenir hunters and hooligans have stripped the brasswork and other valuable parts. Were she in better condition she would no doubt be coveted by enthusiasts resurrecting narrow-gauge lines elsewhere.

Although *Penlee* is rusting away, the railway she once served is busier than ever. Indeed, if the line belonged to British Railways it would have earned a continuous black line on the recently-published map of goods traffic densities: it carries far more than most full-scale West Country branches.

When I paid a visit no fewer than five diesel engines were at work, two shunting and three operating the 'main line' from the quarry loading station to the pier head half a mile or so away, where men tip the contents of the trucks on to a conveyor belt system. Each train was carrying about 40 tons, and ten full and ten empty trains were running each hour while a ship was being loaded. Every few minutes the full train crossed an empty at the loop midway along the main line, and the rattle of rakes of full trucks being pulled and of empty ones being propelled over worn rails and points scarcely ever died away. (1962)

A locomotive of a class which hauled lightly-loaded stopping passenger trains almost unnoticed until two years ago returned to the North Cornwall line on Saturday for a ticker-tape express journey with the most photographed and tape-recorded train so far to run in the West Country. It carried over 100 railway enthusiasts, but many more went to bridges, embankments, and wayside stations to see it pass. Throughout its journey halfway across Devon and Cornwall and back it was greeted like a long-lost friend.

The goddess at the head of the three coaches was No. 120, built in 1899, of the 'T9' or 'Greyhound' class of the London & South Western Railway. Designed by Dugald Drummond, a name which even today inspires awe among lovers of the LSWR, she embodies the best of late Victorian locomotive design, both technical and æsthetic. With her four great driving wheels, her boiler mounted high above her frame, and her eight-wheeled tender veritably symbolising the steam and iron age, she gave a fine boost to the photography industry. Surviving the rest of her class, she is destined for preservation and for assignments such as Saturday's. She is painted in the LSWR pale green livery, though railway enthusiasts and railwaymen alike complained that her colour and lining-out are inaccurate—and, indeed, that she has not been cared for as she might have been. She has been stored out in the open; her fuel was indifferent; and the driver said that though she was a treasure to handle compared with new-fangled machines, she was never the strongest of her class. Driver and fireman —fireman complete with a Victorian moustache, looking as though he might have taken orders from Drummond in person—had to work hard to keep to schedule. . . .

Padstow station, the farthest outpost of the Southern, its quays, fish sheds and array of sidings built in aid of the local economy now practically unused, had a few busy moments while No. 120 shunted her train clear of a local passenger service and then went to the turntable to turn round using her own steam. The enthusiasts surged across the track to watch and shouted to each other as they tried to take pictures not cluttered with human beings in the foreground. And so from Padstow back to Wadebridge and up the spine of Devon and Cornwall, passing several near-empty trains in the opposite direction to Okehampton and Exeter. (1963) (Picture page 110.)

NOTES AND ACKNOWLEDGMENTS

PART ONE

How It Began and *The Age of Toys*. These are abbreviated versions of the first parts of *Paddington to Seagood*: *The Story of a Model Railway* (Chapman & Hall, 1947). As in other extracts from this book, the original text has been slightly adapted to avoid the necessity for connecting commentary and footnotes.

Six Changes. From *Autobiography*: *1891-1941* (Chapman & Hall, 1946). Some years ago I revisited Redbrook-on-Wye and then saw a Dean 0—6—0 shunting the goods at mid-day as I had watched it half a century ago. Now there are no trains in the Wye Valley, which to me seems sadly bereft. Nor can the Valley itself be seen to such excellent advantage as it could from the railway.

Cross-Country Journeys. This first appeared in the *Manchester Guardian* and was reprinted in *Calm Weather*: *a Volume of Essays* (Chapman & Hall, 1930). As the reader will have guessed, it was written with tongue in cheek. The new efficiency, desirable for its own sake, was robbing our railways of the pattern dear to me from childhood. The irony of 'progress' is reflected in the fact that my son has cause to lament the passing of the very things whose *introduction* I regretted! Except on summer Saturdays, long-distance expresses are no longer to be seen at the shrine of Shakespeare.

A Corner of Essex. Part of an essay that first appeared in the *British Weekly* and was then included in *Calm Weather*.

Rationalisation. Extract from *The Master-Light*: *Letters to David* (Allen & Unwin, 1932).

The Hole. From *Paddington to Seagood*. The Hertfordshire 'village' was Harpenden, and the branch railway line (now closed) was that to Hemel Hempstead.

Temple Meads. First published in the *Methodist Recorder*, then included in *Window in the West*: *Essays and Sketches*

(Epworth Press, 1954).

Nostalgia. This poem, with coloured illustrations by Brockbank, appeared as a double-paged spread in *Punch Christmas Almanack* for 1948. It was included in the writer's *Selected Poems* (Allen & Unwin, 1951).

PART TWO

A Signal Success. Written early in 1963. The incident described happened when many Londoners were being re-evacuated following the first V1 raids. The station was South Molton on the Taunton-Barnstaple branch. Pannier-tank locomotives were not usually used on this line, but one was pressed into service on this occasion as shown in the drawing.

A Cornish Byway. Appeared in *The Western Morning News* in 1953. The author was one of the first railway enthusiasts to visit this byway, but many pilgrimages have been made in recent years, and shots of the Beattie tanks—withdrawn in 1962—taking water at the water tower supplied by a stream have a place of honour in many photographic collections. The author's picture, on page 92, also appears as the frontispiece in *A Regional History of the Railways of Great Britain: Volume One, The West Country* (Phoenix House, 1960, reprinted 1963).

Narrow Gauge to Killybegs. This was written as a 'Publishers' Postscript' to Dr E. M. Patterson's *The County Donegal Railways* published by the author's firm of David & Charles in 1962.

The CK & P. A chapter from *Lake District Transport Report, The Findings Of The Lake District Transport Enquiry* (David & Charles, 1961). Sponsored by Sir Patrick Hamilton, chairman of the North Western Transport Users' Consultative Committee, and backed financially by three county councils and the Lakes Planning Board, the Enquiry was the most ambitious independent investigation so far made into public transport arrangements in Britain. The forecast made in the last paragraph of the chapter proved correct. At the time of writing the double-track sections and signalling arrangements are still unchanged. Under the Beeching Plan, the line is again now threatened with closure.

Steam's Indian Summer. Written early in 1962.

Vital But Not Viable. The introduction to *North Devon Railway Report, The Findings Of The North Devon Railway Enquiry* (David & Charles, 1963).

Stress And Storm. The account of the 'funeral' appeared in *The Western Morning News* on 31 December 1962.

The Burden of the Past. Extracts from *The Rural Transport Problem,* the first full-length book on the subject. (Routledge & Kegan Paul, 1963.)

Railway Publishing. Written by the author as a publisher for the *Journal* of the Railway and Canal Historical Association.

The authors are grateful to the publishers and the proprietors and editors of the newspapers mentioned above for permission to reprint material contained in this book. Some use has also been made of material first published in *The Independent* (Plymouth), *John O'London's,* the *Model Railway News, Modern Transport,* and the *Western Evening Herald,* and the authors are likewise grateful to their proprietors and editors.

THE ILLUSTRATIONS

With the exception of that on page 172, all the sketches have been drawn specially for this book by Kenneth Lindley. Many people have helped in the selection of the other pictures. Specific acknowledgments are:

Page 25, *top* British Railways, *bottom* Ian L. Wright and Northampton Museum; page 26, *top* and *bottom* P. Gray, *middle* Roger Sellick; page 27, *top* W. A. Camwell, *bottom* Derek Cross; page 28, *top* J. I. C. Boyd, from *The Isle of Man Railway, middle* Festiniog Railway, *bottom* Ravenglass &

Eskdale Railway; page 37, Leicester Museum; page 55, *top* British Railways, *bottom Bristol Evening Post*; page 56, *top* British Railways, *bottom* John Marshall; page 73, *bottom The Western Morning News*; page 75, P. Gray; page 91, P. Gray; page 109, *top* and *bottom* P. Gray, *middle* Peter F. Bowles; page 110, *top* Roger Sellick, *middle left The Western Morning News, middle right* Albert J. Fellows; page 127, *top The Western Morning News, middle* and *bottom* British Railways; page 128, A. Richardson; page 146, Messrs Bassett-Lowke Limited. The pictures on pages 172 to 177 are taken from books published by David & Charles. The remaining plates are from the author's collection.

INDEX

Italic figures at end of entries denote illustrations

THE END